END

"With so many books on prayer, a new one needs a fresh perspective on the subject to distinguish itself from others. Jed succeeds by helping us see prayer as a child talking to his or her heavenly Father in simple, childlike ways. And like any good book on prayer, *21 Days to Childlike Prayer* makes you *want* to pray."

Donald S. Whitney, author of *Spiritual Disciplines for the Christian Life* and *Praying the Bible*

"I'm at an advantage as I read *21 Days to Childlike Prayer;* I've watched the author, year after year, put every word into action. This book is an accessible, simple tool to help transform your prayer life *and* your heart. You will grow in your prayer life, and you will also grow in your faith, love, and trust of your heavenly Father, who bids you come to Him as His child."

Trillia Newbell, author of *Sacred Endurance, Fear and Faith,* and *Creative God, Colorful Us*

"This is not a book telling you how badly you should feel for how little you pray. It's also not a book telling you how to become an expert in prayer. To the contrary, Jed shows us practically how we can overcome our hesitancies and approach our Father not as fearful applicants but as beloved children."

Russell Moore, *Christianity Today*

"I rarely see a pastor passionate about prayer. But that's what you get in Jed. He is on the front lines of life and has learned how to weave prayer into the fabric of his life. What makes this book so helpful is he gives specific and concrete steps for putting into practice the deep structures of a praying life. This book will get you moving closer to your heavenly Father!"

Paul E. Miller, author of *A Praying Life*

"This book is simple, practical, and most of all, doable! If you want to learn how to pray to a gracious and loving heavenly Father, this can help you get started."

Daniel L. Akin, president, Southeastern Baptist Theological Seminary, Wake Forest, NC

"I had the privilege of calling Jed my pastor when we lived in Tennessee. His sermons were special and every Sunday, my husband or I would say, 'That is a man who prays.' You could see it in his preaching, in his family, and in the way he lives. *21 Days to Childlike Prayer* is excellent—clear, humble, and helpful, from a man who preaches what he practices."

Scarlet Hiltibidal, AfraidOfAllTheThings.com

"This is a poignant, purposeful, and practical book on approaching prayer with a child-like perspective. Prayer is often the most neglected discipline, and this is a refreshing reminder to embrace God with our B-E-S-T. If you need a boost to your prayer life, this book is a helpful guide that will prompt you to come to our 'heavenly Dad' with expectancy and anticipation!"

Matt Carter, lead pastor, Sagemont Church, Houston, TX

"There are books on prayer that teach you to pray, but there are very few that compel you to pray; this work accomplishes both. With relevant illustrations, substantive and practical instruction, and a call to devotion in prayer, one leaves from this book with more than a short stint of 21 days of prayer; they are entered into a lifetime of prayer. It is one of the most encouraging books on prayer that I've read."

Lemanuel R. Williams, deputy director, Peacemakers

"Most of us struggle with prayer. One reason is that we overcomplicate it. In this book, Jed demystifies prayer and gives us a road map to regular, fruitful, childlike, God-glorifying prayer. If you want to grow in your prayer life, buy this book, and for the next 21 days, commit yourself to the daily readings and exercises. Doing this won't make you perfect in prayer, but it will make prayer more permanent in your life."

Juan R. Sanchez, senior pastor, High Pointe Baptist Church, Austin, TX

"As a pastor and seminary professor, I've had many occasions to lead in prayer, but Jed, my pastor, led me to fresh and stronger application of what I knew. He pressed us to identify, with childlike faith, very particular and improbable items for which we might ask God's provision. I took up the challenge, and, out of the blue, the Lord said yes through a totally unforeseen opportunity. The timing and specificity showed His hand clearly. God could have said no, and that would have been fine, but at least I would have known it was not for want of asking that the door remained closed."

Mark Coppenger, retired professor of Christian philosophy and ethics, Southwestern Baptist Theological Seminary, Fort Worth, TX

"The specific answers to prayers my family prayed when I was a child are now a legacy of God's faithfulness that I pass on to my own children, yet I sometimes struggle with what Jed calls 'Vague Prayer Syndrome.' This book has challenged me to come to my Father with specificity like a child. Both biblically faithful and wonderfully practical, I believe it is perfect for anyone who wants to grow in prayerfulness but doesn't know how to start."

Catherine Parks, author of *Empowered: How God Shaped 11 Women's Lives*

21 DAYS
TO
CHILDLIKE
PRAYER

JED COPPENGER

HARVEST HOUSE PUBLISHERS
EUGENE, OREGON

Published in association with Don Gates of the literary agency The Gates Group, www.thegatesgroup.com

Cover design by Faceout Studio

Cover photo © Ms. Moloko, Atishok, Skeleton Icon/Shutterstock

Interior design by Aesthetic Soup

For bulk, special sales, or ministry purchases, please call 1-800-547-8979. Email: Customerservice@hhpbooks.com

21 Days to Childlike Prayer
Copyright © 2022 by Jedidiah Coppenger
Published by Harvest House Publishers
Eugene, Oregon 97408
www.harvesthousepublishers.com

ISBN 978-0-7369-8412-6 (pbk.)
ISBN 978-0-7369-8413-3 (eBook)

Library of Congress Control Number: 2021937784

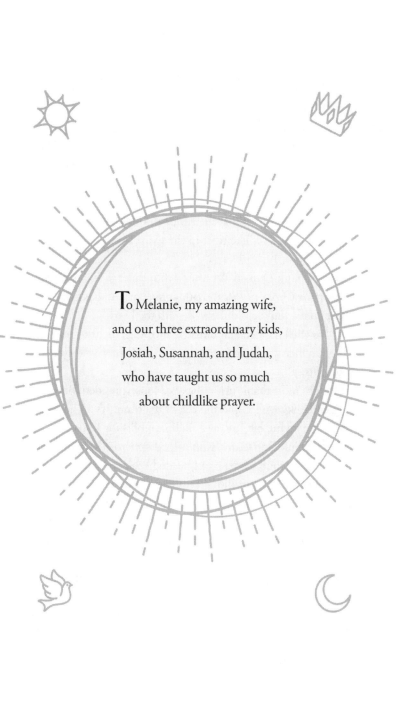

To Melanie, my amazing wife,
and our three extraordinary kids,
Josiah, Susannah, and Judah,
who have taught us so much
about childlike prayer.

ACKNOWLEDGMENTS

It's hard to find the words to express my gratitude for so many people whom God has used to point me to Jesus and what it looks like to follow him with childlike faith, wonder, and trust. Shortening the list to fit this page is, without a doubt, an impossibility.

But I'd like to start by thanking my parents, Mark and Sharon Coppenger, who have followed Jesus faithfully through the ups and downs of life. God used their childlike trust in the worst times to draw me to the Savior.

I'd like to thank Donald Whitney, who, through his book *Spiritual Disciplines of the Christian Life* and our conversations, has had an incredible impact on my daily, childlike walk with the Lord.

Trillia Newbell has been an unusual encouragement to me. I'll never forget the way her words and efforts moved this project forward at strategic moments.

I couldn't be more thankful for Harvest House, president Bob Hawkins, Steve Miller, Becky Miller, and the rest of the team. It's an honor to partner with such a joyful, biblical, and skillful publishing house.

I'd like to thank Don Gates, who helped the project find a home, providing me with encouragement and needed coaching along the way. It's great to have an agent who enjoys tacos and a good time as much as me.

I can't put into words the heartfelt love and gratitude I have for the people of Redemption City Church, who have taught me and walked with me through so much. Thank you for your patience and for being a people of childlike, specific prayer.

And most of all, I'd like to thank my wife, Melanie. No one has prayed more, encouraged more, loved more, sacrificed more to help me with this project. Melanie, you're the greatest answer to a specific prayer that I've ever prayed.

CONTENTS

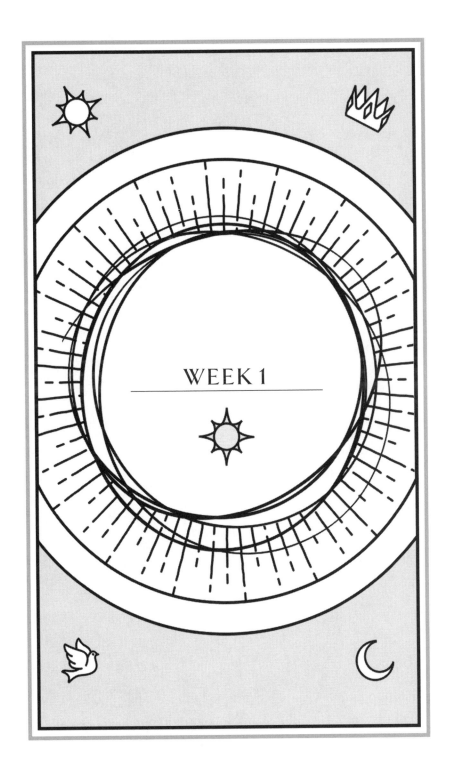

WEEK 1

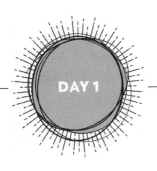

INTRODUCTION
AND FOUR FOUNDATIONAL
CHILDLIKE PRAYER PRINCIPLES

*If you want to judge how well a person understands
Christianity, find out how much he makes of the thought
of being God's child, and having God as his Father. If this
is not the thought that prompts and controls his worship
and prayers and his whole outlook on life, it means that
he does not understand Christianity very well at all.*

J.I. PACKER

*I lift up my eyes to the hills.
From where does my help come?
My help comes from the LORD,
who made heaven and earth.*

PSALM 121:1-2

I love talking about prayer. I get energized helping people who have never had a meaningful, daily, purpose-focusing, peace-producing, exciting prayer life learn how to start one. My days get brighter when I hear stories of specific answers to prayer from people who can't believe "this thing (prayer) works!" Prayer is my passion.

But most people don't feel this way about prayer. For most Christians I know, prayer is the last thing they'd choose to read a book about. Someone would have to talk them into picking up a book like this. You might even know that prayer is something you *should* do, but you just never end up actually doing it.

For what it's worth, if I just described you or something that's close to you, I understand the struggle. I'm not looking self-righteously down on you. I get it. Because prayerlessness was the norm for most of my Christian life. The gap between what I knew I *should* be doing and what I was actually doing was vast.

And this prayer gap that existed in my life wasn't there because I didn't own a lot of books on prayer. I did! My days started without expectant prayer in a house with all kinds of prayer classics. Like you, I also had plenty of access to the Internet's endless resources on prayer. I even studied prayer in seminary. I knew a lot of great quotes that I could share on social media platforms. And I certainly knew that the Bible talked a lot about it, and I could even quote a verse or two on the spot.

But I didn't have a prayer life. Or I should say, I didn't have much of a prayer life. I struggled. And by struggled, I mean I failed and it didn't matter much to me in my day-to-day.

But there remained this uneasiness about my prayerlessness that would show up on the rare occasions that I actually thought about it. I knew that Jesus was all about prayer. I could quote the scriptural commands to pray.

And I certainly was aware of the incredible ways God answered prayers throughout the Bible. A quick look at the lives of Abraham, Joseph, Moses, Joshua, David, Solomon, Nehemiah, Elijah, Daniel, Esther, Deborah, Peter, and Paul highlights the fact that God loves to unleash his stunning power for undeserving people who pray. I wondered if God might still do stuff like that.

Thankful to say, God didn't leave me in my prayerlessness. Unfortunately, it took a lot of pain to close the prayer gap in my life. Early on in the life of the church I started, I went through one of those worst-case scenario after worst-case scenario kind of seasons in life. Mistakes were made, relationships ruined, and the young church that I started was being led by someone who couldn't find his way out of the fog of depression. While what I went through wasn't anything close to what Job went through when he lost everything, my heart felt something of what he felt when he said, "The thing I feared has overtaken me, and what I dreaded has happened to me" (Job 3:25 CSB).

The reason I'm so thankful for that awful season is because, in that season, God changed my life by changing my prayer life. And he changed my view of prayer because he changed my view of him. My problems positioned me to see God in a fresh way that made prayer finally make sense to my busy twenty-first-century life. I learned more about him and, consequently, more about myself. And the more all of these things fell into place, the more I was able to pray in a way that helped me face chaotic situations without a chaotic heart and encounter discouraging circumstances with a heart full of courage. I found my prayer life focusing me and inspiring me, enabling me to take on larger challenges personally and professionally with an inner peaceful steadiness.

I believe I experienced something of what the apostle Paul was talking about in 2 Corinthians 12:10 (CSB), where he said he "delighted" or took "pleasure" in "weaknesses, insults, hardships, persecutions, and in difficulties, for the sake of Christ. For when I am weak, then I am strong." Why would Paul "delight" in those awful things that we all want to run from? Because Paul knew that in those horrible seasons, there was a unique, awesome experience of Jesus that he couldn't experience outside of those seasons. Jesus turns our problems into platforms—platforms where we can experience more of his power, grace, love, wisdom, and direction.

That was true for me in my difficult time. Jesus met me in my nightmare.

One of the greatest guides God used to help me grow through that challenging season was a guy named Paul Miller. He wrote a book called *A Praying Life*, and in it he shared how God used the immense challenges of raising a daughter with Down syndrome to teach him to pray. God used his problems to position him to see and experience Jesus in a way that changed his prayer life.

Over the years, I've recommended his book to as many people as would listen (and I still do!). But I also discovered along the way that God had started writing a unique story in my life that he might want me to share. God seemed to be leading me to tell others what he'd been showing me, what he'd been using in other people's lives—something that might help individuals, families, friends, coworkers, teams, groups, churches go through a journey together that would enable them to become more joyful, courageous, peaceful, purposeful, loving, and productive.

Over the past several years, I have seen prayerless people start to pray and see actual specific answers to prayer over and over. From the gift of millions of dollars of land, to raises at work, to book deals, to DMV lines moving quickly (If God can do that, he can do anything!), to greater experiences with God, to the conscience of lost people—just to name a few—we have seen thousands and thousands of specific answers to prayer. As people learned to pray, Jesus became real to them in their day-to-day living in a way that he had never been. And when Jesus became real in that way, peace became possible to them in places they never thought it could, joy was present in their hearts even in the face of potential failures, and hope marked their outlook as they attempted great things. They found more of the life that Jesus died to purchase than they ever thought possible.

I'm praying that God would use this book to do the same for you as well. I'm praying that Jesus becomes so real to you that you talk to him in prayer every day, that you see specific answers to prayer, and that you too feel comfortable helping others experience Jesus through prayer.

Am I promising that God will answer all of your prayers like you want? Absolutely not. While we have seen thousands upon thousands of specific answers to prayer, we have seen tens of thousands of specific *nos* to prayers. More of our requests are denied than are granted. Why? As we'll see this week, not because God doesn't love us, but because it's not what's best for us. His *nos* are always an "I have something better that you can't see."

I believe that 21 days from now anyone who reads, engages in the process, and applies what they learn in this book will be able to pray in a way that enables them to experience God's power in their day-to-day life as we have. That's right, anyone. Why? Because the secret to a "daily, life-giving, see-specific-answers-to-prayer" prayer life isn't found in becoming more spiritually sophisticated. It only requires that we become more childlike.

When Jesus taught his disciples to pray in what has now become his famous "Lord's Prayer," he pointed them toward the Father-child relationship. "Our Father…" Jesus tells his disciples to pray (Matthew 6:9). Why? Because the nature of the relationship determines the nature of the communication. Kids talk to their parents in a way that you can't talk to their parents. Right? Jesus doesn't want his listeners to think they need to become superstar Christians in order to pray like he wants them to pray. Jesus just wants them to start acting like a child.

Over the next 21 days, I'm going to do my best to take you on a journey into childlike prayer. I want to help you learn what I learned without having to go through what I went through. When we embrace childlike prayer, we find ourselves in a new story where anything is possible, where we always get what's best, where miracles happen every day, and where problems are opportunities for a greater experience of Jesus.

I'd encourage you to do your best to read it with someone else. Whether it's a close friend, a family member, a team, a group, a staff, or a church, any group that pursues childlike prayer together will see more of Jesus than they would if they just pursued it on their own. When Jesus started out his instructional prayer with an "our," he was pointing us toward a place where our community—whatever size or type of community that is—knows of specific, awesome answers to prayers that have happened in their midst. Just as Israel and the early church had unique, inspiring, faith-feeding stories about how God answered their prayers, Jesus wants your friend group, church group, work group, family, or whatever your group looks like to have unique, inspiring, faith-feeding stories.

Let me challenge you to come up with a "Top 10" requests list. If you're going through this book with others, make two "Top 10" prayer request lists, one public and one private. These requests can be problems that are pressing in on you right now as you read. They may come from any area of life. They can also be plans that you would love to see fulfilled. They don't have to be spiritual. Any decent dad wants to help his kids in any area of life they are interested in—so long as they're not harmful to them. God is a perfect Father, perfect in love, mercy, generosity, and joy, and he isn't turned off by requests for "nonspiritual" things.

Because I know that many people in our groups are not next-level readers, I've written each chapter in a way that one should be able to read it in ten to fifteen minutes. Add that up over 21 days and it isn't much more time than you'd spend watching a couple of your favorite movies.

This first week, we'll explore the Lord's Prayer. I'll show you that prayer can simply be understood as God's children talking to their heavenly Father about what they think is best. To help remember the key elements that make this communication happen, I've created the following acronym that we'll unpack over the course of this first week:

FOUR FOUNDATIONAL CHILDLIKE PRAYER PRINCIPLES

B—Believe God can do anything.
E—Embrace your childlike identity.
S—Specify your requests.
T—Trust God to do what's best with your requests.

Start praying that God would help you incorporate these key elements of prayer into your life. To help, I'll include this acronym at the end of each day's reading, serving as a daily prompt to pray like God's child.

The second week, you will learn how to put the principles you learned in week one into practice. You'll learn about the "Six Childlike Prayer Practices," which are necessary to make this experience with Christ more than a 21-day experience. Don't make this journey the finish; make it the start of something new and life-changing.

During the third week, we'll continue to think more deeply about the Lord's Prayer and how it reveals five characteristics that mark the blood-bought identity of every child of God. Learned into your heart, while also pointing your attention to the most strategic prayers God's children can pray. Here, you'll learn "Five Specific Childlike Identity Prayers." Christians who learn to pray these prayers will see how childlike prayer positions them to live the life their heavenly Father created them to live each day. They'll learn to change their world in just a few moments at the start of every day.

For 21 days, step away from your phone a little more, turn off the TV a little sooner, and follow God into childlike prayer. What kind of stories of answered prayer might you have three months from now if you really embrace this challenge? What might God do in your relationships, work, group, or church if you said no to a few things over the next 21 days so that you could say yes to this 21-day challenge?

I'm praying that God would answer specific prayer requests for each person that goes through this journey. I'm asking God to surprise you in ways that lift your heart, enable you to take on the impossible, unite your life more meaningfully with those you go through this with, and trust God with all your problems and plans.

DAILY REFLECTION

When and where will you read the daily text and engage in its exercises?

_____

If you're going through this journey with a group, how will you talk about it? Daily? Weekly? Over lunch? Breakfast? Through text thread?

_____

_____

What are the reasons for your "prayer gap"?

_____

What are you putting on your "Top 10" prayer lists publicly? What about your private "Top 10" prayer requests?

1. _____

2. _____

3. _____

4. _____

5. _____

6. _____

7. _____

8. _____

9. _____

10. _____

DAILY PRAYER

God, I need your help to make it through this 21-Day Childlike Prayer Challenge. Will you cause me to get off to a great start? Will you help me identify and overcome the obstacles that get in the way? Will you cause my heart to believe that there are no prayer requests too small for you to care about, and that there are no prayer requests too big for you to handle in a moment without any effort? Enable me to believe you can truly do anything. Help me embrace a childlike identity, specify my prayer requests, and trust you to do what's best with my requests. With the psalmist, we pray, "Let your work be shown to your servants" (Psalm 90:16). While we don't know what your answers to these requests will be, thank you for always doing what's best for your children. Amen.

DAY 2

BELIEVE GOD CAN DO ANYTHING

*Oddly enough, many people struggle to learn how to pray
because they are focusing on praying, not on God.*

PAUL MILLER

*When the LORD restored the fortunes of Zion,
we were like those who dream.
Then our mouth was filled with laughter,
and our tongue with shouts of joy;
then they said among the nations,
"The LORD has done great things for them."*

PSALM 126:1-2

M y oldest son, Josiah, was unusually quiet on the ride home from baseball practice. He was still at that age where baseball was basically a bunch of cute kids running around in the dirt, ignoring parents whose patience was running short. It was the best of times. It was the worst of times.

Normally, on the ride home, Josiah would tell me what his teammates were talking about. A new joke he learned. How he thought he played. A funny noise he heard. Smells he smelled. And other interesting details on which five-year-old boys tend to focus. Not this time. He was dead silent.

But as we turned into the neighborhood, he finally leaned forward and said, "Dad, you threw the baseball *all* the way from first base to third base in the air!" Looking into the rearview mirror with a bit of a curious smile, I said, "I sure did, bud." He slowly leaned back and began to smile with the kind of "lost in the moment" smile you have when you see something awesome you've never seen before. Then he said, "Dad, is there anything you can't do?"

I took another quick look in the rear-view mirror to see if he was joking, but he wasn't. He was just smiling, staring out the window, enjoying, if for even a moment, the thought that his dad could do anything. It's like he was looking at the world differently. From his view, there were as many possibilities in this new world as there were mountains in the Rockies—more than you can see, more than you can fathom.

That's childlike faith.

Childlike faith happens when the children of God see God for who he really is. This perspective is so life-giving that it disorients you the moment it happens. When you see his unmatchable power, unsearchable knowledge, and unending love, hope surges through your heart like a lightning bolt.

I imagine that same kind of feeling was felt by the Israelites after they walked out of Egypt for the first time as free men and women. Even though they had been backed up to the Red Sea with the world's most powerful military—the Egyptian army—approaching, God made a way for them to pass through the Red Sea. It marked every Israelite after.

Daniel, no doubt, and those aligned with Daniel felt it freshly in their heart as Daniel was helped out of the lions' den where he spent the night making history by being the first person ever to come out of that den unharmed.

You have to think that Shadrach, Meshach, and Abednego certainly felt that my-God-can-do-anything childlike faith when they walked out of the fiery furnace they were thrown into because they wouldn't turn from their God.

Lazarus knew what it was like to walk in childlike faith after Jesus brought him back from the dead.

Peter and those praying for Peter knew what it was like to believe in the God of the impossible, especially after being escorted out of a Roman prison the night before he was to be executed for being a Christian.

The Bible is filled with examples of God unleashing his power on behalf of his undeserving children. These are just a few. I bet they all had a smile like Josiah had that day, and perhaps a similar look in their eyes, the one that comes from the childlike belief that their God could do anything.

And here is the important thing to notice: These events didn't just happen to occur; they were important enough to be recorded in the Bible. Why? Our God described those events in Scripture for us so that we'd have that same feeling as we made our way through each day, the one Josiah had that day when he saw me do the impossible and throw the ball all the way across the infield.

That's one of the reasons why Jesus starts teaching his disciples about prayer by directing their focus to God's identity. He says, "Pray then like this: Our Father in heaven…" (Matthew 6:9). Jesus wants us to know exactly who we are talking to in prayer from the very start. Because your view of God will determine your view of prayer. Your view of prayer reveals your view of God.

Paul Miller insightfully writes, "Oddly enough, many people struggle to learn how to pray because they are focusing on praying, not on God."[1] When you're having trouble with your prayer life, one of the main places you need to check is your view of God.

J.I. Packer agrees. He says, "People who know their God are before anything else people who pray…If there is little energy for such prayer, and little consequent practice of it, this is a sure sign that as yet we scarcely know our God."[2]

As we saw on the first day, when Jesus teaches us about prayer, he points our attention to the Father-child relationship. Because God is "our Father," he is "eagerly willing" to unleash his infinite power for the good of his kids.

When Jesus first spoke these words next to the Sea of Galilee, it wasn't common to speak of God as a father. There were no songs about a "Good, Good Father," and there were certainly no pieces of wall art in Jesus' childhood home that said anything about a heavenly Father. At that time, people employed many titles to describe God, but they didn't say "Father." That would have felt presumptuous.

Jesus is showing us a new way to relate to God, one that he alone, through his life, death, and resurrection, makes possible. Jesus is taking people who are far from God and turning them into family.

Slow down for a second and think about that term *father*. Jesus, of course, knew that there are bad fathers. Perhaps you had one of them. But Jesus also knew that the normal father is someone who tries to do what's best for his kids. Even if he is limited, he is willing to help.

So if normal dads want to do what's best for their kids, how much more should we expect the perfect, heavenly Father to always do what's best for his kids? Jesus made this point to another audience filled with good folks like you and me. He said, "If you then, who are evil, know how to give good gifts to your children, how much more will your Father who is in heaven give good things to those who ask him!" (Matthew 7:11).

Jesus starts his teaching on prayer by clarifying how he wants his listeners to view the God to whom they are speaking. Because your view of God will determine your practice of prayer. And your practice of prayer will reveal your view of God.

But Jesus doesn't just tell us that we are talking to a God who is "Father," so we know he is willing to help. He also tells us that we are talking to a God who is "in heaven," so we know that he is able to help.

Over the years, some folks have told me that they thought the phrase "in heaven" made God seem distant. But that's not why Jesus used that phrase. "In heaven" isn't meant to communicate distance; it's meant to communicate competence. Because God is "in heaven," he is unstoppable.

Jesus is connecting the identity of the one we are speaking to in prayer with the God who "is in heaven and does whatever he pleases" (Psalm 115:3 csb); the one for whom "all things are possible" (Mark 10:27); the one who easily brought about every miracle we find in Scripture. His power is unmatched and unending. He's unstoppable. And he never gets tired or needs a break when he does more in a moment than we can do in a lifetime.

Jesus wants us to know from the very beginning that we are speaking to a God who is endlessly capable and eagerly willing to do what's best for his kids. He wants us to have so high a view of God's power that we really believe he can make a difference in our lives, inner thought life, health, relationships, finances, work life, and more, and a high enough view of

God's love that we really believe he is eagerly working to do what's best in our lives.

Do you view God like this?

Most of us don't. We don't believe God can do absolutely anything. Sure, we don't say that. But that's what our prayerlessness proclaims. How do you know what your heart really thinks about God's ability or willingness to help you with your problems and plans? Look at your prayer life. If you are daily asking God for help, you have a heart that believes in God's ability and love. If you aren't asking, you don't.

When we say that we're too busy to pray, our lives are saying, "It is more productive for me to get to work than to ask God to help me with my work." That's not just a problem because we didn't pray. It shows that we aren't seeing who God is and what he can do rightly. It also reveals that we don't understand who we are either (but we'll talk about this more in the next chapter).

Jesus designed our prayer life to change our perspective. And at the heart of this change is a change about how we view God, from thinking he is unable or unwilling to help to knowing he is able and willing.

Jesus says that if you want to learn how to pray, you need start by battling to believe in the right God. He wants to make sure that you're thinking about the right God. The same God who could handle Egypt, Babylon, and Rome is present and able to handle your situations too. So sit back, smile, and as you look at your day, in your heart whisper to yourself, "My Father can do anything."

When you are growing in your belief that God can do anything, you need to grow in your belief in his power, his love, his grace, and his wisdom. When you believe in his power, you ask him to help you with specific situations in your day. When you believe in his love, you don't hesitate to ask for anything on your heart. When you believe in his wisdom, you trust him to do what's best.

The best place to foster this perspective is by looking to the gospel. The gospel is the good news that Jesus saves those who put their trust in him because he lived the perfect life they failed to live, died the sinner's death they deserved to die, and was raised from the dead—showing that his payment on the cross was accepted.

Have you asked Jesus to be your Savior and Lord? He always answers that prayer yes!

When we place our hope in his finished work, Jesus says that we are *justified*, which means "declared righteous" in God's courtroom. And we are adopted into Christ's family. Every adopted child of God is given the Spirit who uses the Word of God, the people of God, and the situations in our lives to make us more like Jesus.

And one of the key ways we are transformed is by moving from being prayerless to prayerful. How? By changing the way we view God as we think about the gospel truths. Because God the Son, Jesus, was willing to die on the cross for sinners, we can never question his love. Because God the Son, Jesus, walked out of the grave, we should never question his power. And because no one foresaw all of this happening the way that it did, we should never question his wisdom.

The greater God becomes in your eyes, the more you will feel childlike faith welling up in your heart. This is a daily battle. Some days you will find it easier to see God in all his bigness, and other days you will struggle. But, as we'll see in a few days, specific requests are one of the key ways to foster this childlike faith. Because specific requests lead to specific answers. And when God answers us specifically we see him in a way we never would without those specific requests. Specificity leads to visibility.

Let me share one of my favorite specific answers to prayer. I started talking with a couple, Frank and Francis Ingraham, about the congregation I lead, Redemption City Church, and about purchasing property for our church from them. They owned a large farm—a farm that I grew up working on. They were heroes to me. And they were at the end of their life, and the land would most likely be sold and turned into neighborhoods.

So, I asked Mr. Frank if they might be open to our church purchasing a piece of their property so that the things he invested in us all those years ago could continue in the life of a local church, long after they were gone, in the same fields we had worked in.

They were open to it, so we started a conversation that lasted several years. They wanted the church to buy an amount of land I thought was too much for us to afford. They didn't need the money. They simply wanted to help the church avoid getting landlocked, which might require us to move at some point. They believed in the church and wanted to see it flourish.

I wanted the church to buy a much smaller amount of land, something much closer to what we could afford and would still allow for us to grow a great deal if the Lord blessed us.

So we went back and forth, having a lot of fun along the way.

And then one October, I started praying a simple prayer: "God, please cause them to give us their land." That was it. That's what I prayed.

Nine months later, sitting at their dining room table with a friend, Frank told me that they would like for our church to buy the amount that we felt comfortable buying and that they would give us the rest that they wanted us to have. That meant we bought 7.6 acres and they gave us 23.30 acres! In our area, one of the wealthiest counties in America, this was unheard of.

I didn't offer an eloquent prayer. God doesn't need great prayers to do great things. I wasn't living a perfect life. God doesn't need great people praying to do great things.

When I left their house, you'd better believe I floated to the car. As my friend drove us away, I looked out the window the same way Josiah did that day coming home from baseball—not wondering but believing, there's nothing my heavenly Father can't do.

DAILY REFLECTION

On a scale of one to ten, with one being "I don't believe God can do anything" and ten being "I genuinely believe God can do anything," what number would you give God right now in your life? Why? What about your group, family, church, team? Why?

If you were at a ten on that scale, what do you think your prayer life would look like each day? Why?

DAILY PRAYER PROMPT

B—Believe God can do anything.

E—Embrace your childlike identity.

S—Specify your requests.

T—Trust God to do what's best with your requests.

DAILY PRAYER

God, grow my capacity to see you for who you really are. Help me see your power, love, and wisdom in such a way that my heart feels toward you like Jed's son Josiah felt toward him in the moment he described. Cause me to be more affected by your stunning presence, person, and plans than I am by the brokenness of this world. Help me to look at my problems with your resources in view, my failures with your gracious love, and my fears with your calming presence and unstoppable promises. Help me walk in childlike faith throughout this day. Cause our hearts to say with the psalmist, "Our God is in heaven and does whatever he pleases," and at the same time, that it pleases you to do what's best for us (Psalm 115:3 CSB; Romans 8:28). Amen.

Take a few moments and write out a prayer below that asks God to help you have a high enough view of him and his competencies that you start to ask him for help.

_____

_____

_____

_____

_____

_____

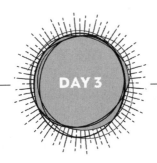

DAY 3

EMBRACE YOUR CHILDLIKE IDENTITY

*Being born again happens in an instant. Learning
to live as a child of God takes a lifetime.*

DERWIN GRAY

*O LORD, my heart is not lifted up;
my eyes are not raised too high;
I do not occupy myself with things
too great and too marvelous for me.
But I have calmed and quieted my soul,
like a weaned child with its mother;
like a weaned child is my soul within me.*

PSALM 131:1-2

I don't remember hearing the door open, but I woke up to the sound of it closing. Just about that same, startling, middle-of-the-night, there's-someone-in-my-room moment, I heard the words from one of my kids break through the 2:00 a.m. silence in my bedroom. "I can't find my night-night," she said. Her "night-night" was her blanket and, apparently, someone had come in and stolen it.

Like just about every parent I know, I slowly stumbled out of bed and into her bedroom, looking for the secret to my seven-year-old's good night's sleep. Accessing my unique parental skills, I started by turning on the light. Ah, sure enough, it was in her bed, literally right next to her. She happily said, "My night-night!" grabbed it, and got under her covers.

All of my kids, like most kids, have done this kind of thing more than once. Sometimes it's their night-night, other times it's a bad dream. Whatever the reasons might be for their middle-of-the-night meetings, they always feel important to them.

Of course, these reasons feel so important to them that it has never dawned on them that maybe, just maybe, my sleep might be important too. They've never quietly entered my room, gently awakened me with a "sorry to wake you, especially since you've had such a long day (or have a big meeting tomorrow, or I know I haven't been good today), but…" There's no concern for my condition, just their problem.

Or, to continue, when we've found the blanket, I've never heard one of my kids say, "I'm so sorry I woke you up, especially when I could have just rolled over and checked the other side where I was lying down. *Thank you* so much for helping me! I can't believe how quickly you left the comfort of your bed to come help me." Or anything like that.

Children naturally assume that their parents are concerned with what they are concerned with. Kids have no trouble knocking down doors in the middle of the night for the smallest problems. And kids can do this in a way that no one else can. Adults that come into other adult's rooms in the middle of the night aren't helped; they're arrested.

And, of course, this middle-of-the-night boldness isn't the only example of the unique ways a child relates to a parent. Whether it's at a local restaurant, on a sports field, at church, or anywhere else, children relate to their parents in a way that no one else can.

The reason children can be so bold with their parents in these early stages of life is that they are so dependent on their parents. Kids can't prepare their food, cut their food, use the bathroom properly, or things like this. They need help from their parents in all kinds of areas of life and at all hours. Childlike boldness is rooted in childlike dependency.

That's why it's so important, as we think about how Jesus starts his teaching on prayer, that we don't just focus on God's identity as Father, but also on our identity as children. When we really grasp that Jesus' Father is "Our Father," we realize that means we are his children. Jesus wants his listeners to pray, and in order for that to happen, they have to embrace a childlike identity.

This childlike identity changes the way we view prayer because it changes the way we view our relationship with God. The nature of communication is determined by the nature of the people communicating. And the child-parent conversation is a unique communication channel, one marked by dependency and boldness.

Childlike boldness doesn't hesitate to ask our awesome heavenly Father for something as small as "our daily bread." We have the childlike boldness that enables us to "draw near to the throne of grace" in our time of need (Hebrews 4:16), not just "varsity spiritual needs" but any needs.

We don't have any trouble believing sinful parents like us actually care about their kid's needs. Yet, when we're honest with ourselves, we often have trouble believing that our sinless heavenly Father actually cares about our needs. There are a lot of truths about our triune, infinite God that are hard to wrap our mind around, but it seems quite simple to affirm that "more loving" and "more holy" doesn't mean less caring.

Needs are things like help with key decisions, money situations, relationships, tension, work problems and plans, and more. Needs are anything that you need God's help with. For those keeping score, that's everything.

Do you have that "middle of the night march into my parents' room for a non-emergency" type of boldness?

Oftentimes, we don't.

The reasons why we don't are many. For some of us, we don't embrace our identity as God's children because we aren't God's children. We've never come to the place in our lives where we've surrendered our lives to Jesus' love, turning from being an enemy of God to being a child of God. The gospel shows us that Jesus, the son of God, was treated like an enemy of God on the cross so that the enemies of God, you and I, can be treated like sons and daughters of God. You see, Jesus' life, death, and resurrection are the adoption payment needed to bring us into the family of God forever. It's our role to decide to receive this gift.

Have you received this gift of salvation? If not, there's no access into the Father's gracious presence without it.

But maybe you are already a child of God. Maybe that's not the reason for your prayerlessness. The Bible says that although our standing before

God changes immediately when we receive the gift of salvation by faith, sin is still present in our lives. The penalty has been paid, the power of sin has been broken, but the presence of sin is still ongoing until he returns.

One of the biggest signs of the ongoing presence of sin in our lives is prayerlessness. Prayerlessness says, "I don't need to ask God to help me with my daily life." Another way of talking about this sin of prayerlessness is in terms of pride. Pride is one of those sins that we all know is a problem, but few of us see how it really works in our lives. But it's very simple. Pride doesn't pray. It's the reason why you didn't pray yesterday. Pride doesn't think it needs God's help. Pride thinks that more will be accomplished today by skipping a time of prayer and starting to do the tasks for the day. What's pride sound like? "I'd love to pray, but I don't have time to pray. I have so much to do." That's pride. It's the enemy of embracing a childlike identity. It's the default position for most of God's children. Our prayer life, more than anything else, shows us how much pride is in control of our hearts.

One of the keys to a flourishing, daily prayer life is battling the pride that stands in the way of it. You have to fight to embrace your childlike identity by fighting pride with the words of Jesus, who said, "for apart from me you can do nothing" (John 15:5). Daily prayer happens when we see through the delusions of pride that say we don't need to ask God for help. Prayer is the practical way that we show God and ourselves that we believe Jesus' words in John 15:5.

Do you see how pride causes prayerlessness?

Others show that they struggle to embrace their childlike identity by believing that they need to use a sophisticated strategy to talk to God in prayer. They look at prayer like a sophisticated presentation. In this view, the person praying better say it right. But God doesn't want us to look at prayer like that. No decent parent makes their kids speak to them perfectly in order for them to hear and help.

When you think you have to have a perfect presentation, or even a perfect "record" for the day, for your heavenly Father to hear your prayers, you show you don't understand the greatness of his love and grace. You actually make him seem less loving than any average parent who will do what's best for their kids whether they have had a good day or not, whether they formulate their requests perfectly or not. Parents know what their kids need and they know what they're trying to say. Normal parents don't stop taking care of their kids, wanting to do what's best for their kids, when they aren't asking or living perfectly.

Why would we think God would do less than that?

We, of course, can overreact and think that our lives don't matter at all. If a child is consciously rejecting the parents' clear instructions, parents understand that if they don't address the problem, they are enabling and training the child to do the wrong thing. That's what Jesus' half-brother James was talking about when he told Christians that they weren't receiving answers to prayer, "You ask and do not receive, because you ask wrongly, to spend it on your passions" (James 4:3). Part of embracing a childlike identity is taking seriously the command to do your heavenly Father's will. Will you be perfect? Nope. Jesus knows you're not perfect, that's why he came to save you. But his grace doesn't just change your standing before him; when it is received by faith, it changes the direction of your life. While complete change won't be likely today, genuine change will. If a child of God isn't genuinely trying to do God's will, it hinders their prayers.

That's why Jesus wants his listeners to embrace their childlike identity. If you want to learn to pray, you need to remember who you are. You're God's child, so this daily act that leads to daily prayer marked by boldness is for problems and plans that are big and small. When you truly see who God is as your heavenly Father and who you are as his child, no request is too small for him to hear and help.

I'll never forget one of the moments this truth became real to me. I was on a mission trip in southeast Asia. We were about ten hours past the middle of nowhere, amongst ten unreached, unengaged people groups.

My team had been in the country for several days—long enough for my body to let me know that it didn't appreciate the twelve-hour clock reversal or the lack of sleep that went with it. Turning night into day and day into night wasn't working so well with my midthirties body.

As is the case for me when I don't get sleep for a while, I started to get a cold. Unfortunately, that happened during a small gathering of Christians on a Sunday morning. It was their church gathering. And while it didn't seem like a big deal by the American church's standards, it was momentous by heaven's standards because it was the first gathering like it within that people group.

It was an honor to be there in that room with no electricity, no air conditioning, sweating in the heat. I was listening to someone talk with my Bible open, even though I couldn't understand anything being said.

And then it happened.

My nose started to run. I mean, it started to run like something was chasing it. I tried to do the subtle sniffle, but I needed Kleenex. I looked around the room with desperation in my eyes. I didn't want my only impression on these heroes of the faith to be one with snot running down my face. But there was nothing in sight.

So I prayed, *God, I'm your child, I've got a runny nose. My parents always carried the Kleenex. You made the heavens out of nothing, will you provide me a Kleenex out of nothing?* I kept praying a version of that prayer throughout the service.

As the service was ending, I had my eye on some leaves outside that I was going to make a run for. But before I could go, I felt someone tap me on my arm. I turned around and a lady handed me several Kleenexes.

I couldn't believe it!

That may seem small and silly to you. In many ways, it was. But it was a big deal to me because it represented a life-changing truth. It reminded me what the Bible says over and over: We have a heavenly Father who sees our need, hears our requests, no matter how small, and provides what's best for us, no matter the circumstances. Thankfully, he acts that way toward all of his children.

DAILY REFLECTION

On a scale of one to ten, how would you rate your ability to embrace your childlike identity over the last month? How can that change?

Do you find it harder to embrace childlike dependency or childlike boldness? Why?

_____

_____

DAILY PRAYER PROMPT

B—Believe God can do anything.
E—Embrace your childlike identity.
S—Specify your requests.
T—Trust God to do what's best with your requests.

DAILY PRAYER

Father, help me embrace my childlike identity. Cause me to see through the delusional messages of pride that tell me I don't need to ask for your help. Capture my heart with the truth that you can do more in a moment than I can do in a lifetime. Enable me to see the awesomeness of having access to your throne room. Thank you for sending Jesus to die in my place, purchasing salvation for me. Help me receive that gift by faith. Awaken me to live in that reality. Amen.

_____

_____

_____

_____

SPECIFY YOUR REQUESTS

*Little of the Word with little prayer is death to the spiritual
life. Much of the Word with little prayer gives a sickly
life. Much prayer with little of the Word gives more
life, but without steadfastness. A full measure of the Word
and prayer each day gives healthy and powerful life.*

ANDREW MURRAY

*Teach me to do your will,
for you are my God!
Let your good Spirit lead me
on level ground!*

PSALM 143:10

The older I get, the harder it is for me to come up with a Christmas list,
a birthday list, and a Father's Day list. I'm not sure why it's so hard.
Maybe it's because I buy what I want? Could be that I know that it hurts
the budget? Maybe it's because I want to make sure I ask for the best possible thing, and I don't feel like I have time to really think it through? I'm
not sure. But it's a challenge for me. And from talking with others, it's a
challenge for them.

You know who this isn't a challenge for? Kids. When it is time for them
to come up with a gift list, they have no problem at all. They know exactly

what they want. They have no regard for the budget. None! They don't think about whether or not it is wise for them to use their limited number of presents on that circled option in the magazine they keep showing you. Children know how to ask for stuff and they know how to ask with specificity.

Part of embracing a childlike identity involves embracing specificity. It means that we learn to get specific with prayer requests. And as easy as that sounds, I've found in my life and the lives of those I've helped learn to pray that it is difficult. It takes a good deal of work to help people pray with specificity.

Why? Because most people suffer from what I call the "Vague Prayer Syndrome." The Vague Prayer Syndrome is where you only pray vague prayers. Those vague prayers are so vague that you would never really know if they were answered by God in any meaningful way. These prayers are general prayers that don't create any expectancy for an answer or any excitement when they are answered.

As someone who still battles the Vague Prayer Syndrome, I know what it sounds like—"God be with us today…" Or, "Bless this food…" The great news is that God answered those requests with a yes! How do I know? Because he promised us in Scripture that he would "be with us" and "bless us."

Do you ever pray prayers like this? Do you only pray like this?

It's perfectly fine, of course, to pray these prayers. But when you learn to get specific with your prayer requests, God becomes real in your heart and life in a way that he never would without that specificity. And when he becomes real in your life, when you get a glimpse of him working specifically in your life, it changes you. Fearful people experience peace. Bored people find purpose. Frustrated people find patience. Empty people get filled. People reach goals that are beyond their abilities to bring about.

I've seen it over and over in my life and in the lives of the people around me. Specificity leads to visibility. When we get specific, the invisible God becomes visible in our lives in a way that he wouldn't without that specific request. How do you see the invisible God? Get specific with your requests.

Instead of just saying, "Make today go great," say, "Cause someone to encourage me by the end of the day." Or in regards to that staffing effort at work say, "Provide a new employee this week that we know is the one." Here are some other examples:

God, will you send someone to encourage me in an unusual way today?

God, will you make my encounter with _____ encouraging tonight?

God, will you cause my parents to speak to me more kindly in the mornings this week?

God, will you make my boss affirm my work on this project this week?

God, will you make this physical ailment go away by Thursday?

When God answers those requests, you see God working in your life in ways that lift your heart out of the mess of the world. You start to really believe you have a Father in heaven that cares about you and your problems and plans. You start to awaken the childlike faith your heart was made for.

This is exactly what you see throughout the Bible. When you read the Psalms, you see the psalmists specifically praying that God would deliver them from specific fears, help them overcome a specific enemy, revive their soul, and more. The Israelites prayed for a specific deliverance from Egyptian oppression when they were slaves in Egypt. They prayed specifically for God to save them when they had their backs up against the Red Sea and an Egyptian military coming after them. Daniel specifically asked for deliverance from the lions' den. Jonah prayed specifically for God to get him out of that fish's stomach. Nehemiah prayed that God would help him build a specific wall. And the list could certainly go on. In all of these situations, they knew whether God answered those prayers. And because they were specific with their prayers, when the invisible God answered their prayers, they saw him in a way that they wouldn't have without that specificity. Their specificity led to visibility.

The same is true for us. When you are bold enough to pray specific prayers, you give God an opportunity to become visible—real—in your life in a way he wouldn't be without that specificity.

Ask God to work in specific ways, by specific times, and watch him work. Will he always give you a yes? Of course not. We'll talk about that more in a bit. But for now, you need to become bold enough to pray specifically.

This is one of the reasons that Jesus didn't stop his teaching on prayer with the proper understanding of identity—both God's identity as Father and his followers' identity as children. No, Jesus provides specific prayer pathways on which the Father-child communication flourishes.

We'll spend the rest of today learning about the first one and the following two days learning about the last two. The three primary prayer paths to get specific in prayer involve praying your Bible, your plans, and your problems. We'll start first with the Bible.

PRAYING YOUR BIBLE

Jesus told his listeners to pray, "Hallowed be your name. Your kingdom come, your will be done…" And so often we just repeat his words in our prayers without thinking about their meaning. Remember, Jesus said, "Pray like this," not "Pray exactly these words."

So how do you pray your version of "hallowed be your name, your kingdom come, your will be done…?" The answer to that question becomes obvious when we understand how we know if God's name has been hallowed as it should be, his kingdom has come, and his will has been done. How do we know those things?

The Bible.

Think about it. In the Bible, God tells us how to treat him, advance his kingdom purposes, and do his will. The Bible tells us what kingdom advancement looks like in our hearts, relationships, finances, time management, and all the rest.

But knowing the Bible isn't enough. We need God's help to do God's will. We show that we understand this when we move from simply reading God's Word to praying God's Word. And with over 23,100 verses in the Bible, we have plenty of material to pray.

What's this look like practically? I've found the following to be helpful in my Bible reading:

Read it. As simple as this sounds, this is a radical step. When we read the Word of God, we hear from God. The apostle Paul says that "all Scripture is breathed out by God" (2 Timothy 3:16). The Bible, rightly understood, tells us what God's will is, how his kingdom is advanced, and how to hallow his name.

Think about it. Parents don't want their message to go in one ear and out the other, and neither does God. That's why he tells us to meditate, to think about his Word (Psalm 1:2). Some questions to help you think about a passage can be (to name a few possibilities): What does it say? What jumped out to you the most? What's your favorite part? What did the author mean? How does it apply? How does it connect to Christ? Some days I give more thought than others. The important thing is to give it *some* thought.

Pray it. We need God's help to do God's will. Once you understand what you read, pray what you understand. Ask God to help you, enable you, cause you to follow his Word in the specific situations you anticipate for that day. Ask God to help others to do the same.

Instead of just reading a passage like Philippians 2:3, "Do nothing from selfish ambition or conceit, but in humility count others more significant than yourselves"—and then just going and doing your best, understand that there's more. It's great, but it's not enough.

Rather, you should ask God for help to "count others more significant than yourself." Instead of "others," put specific names in that place and pray it. Ask God to show you areas where you might be driven by "selfish ambition" or "conceit." As you think about what you need to do that day, ask him to help you walk in humility in those activities.

This is just one of many ways where, if you give a Bible passage a little thought and prayer, you will learn how to get specific in your Bible reading. When you do this, you are praying a version of "hallowed be your name, your kingdom come, your will be done." You'll find yourself more engaged in your Bible reading, confessing sin more often in that moment, enabling the life-giving words of God to get into parts of your heart that are in desperate need of it.

As simple as this sounds, this is a terrifying act for the enemy of God's will. Satan does not want God's children asking their heavenly Father to do God's will. The enemy wants God's children to think about their little "kingdoms" without any regard to their heavenly Father's kingdom. If they are going to read the Bible, the enemy only wants them to try to obey it in their strength without asking for help. The enemy hates when God's children pray simple, specific prayers from the Bible.

Do you pray your Bible?

One of the greatest examples in all of Christian history of praying with specificity is George Müller. Readers have enjoyed thousands and thousands of his recorded answers to specific prayers. Why did he pray so much? Well, he pastored, ran a publishing house, and many more things in the mid-1800s in England. He's most famous for his work with orphans. He created an orphanage that made a massive impact in England.

But what many people, even those who are familiar with his story, don't realize about him is that he saw, more than anything else in his life, that his primary job was to be "happy in the Lord." And a key part of this work focused on praying his Bible.

Here's how he described it:

> The first thing I did, after having asked in a few words the Lord's blessing upon His precious Word, was to begin to meditate on the Word of God; searching, as it were, into every verse, to get blessing out of it; not for the sake of the public ministry of the Word; not for the sake of preaching on what I had meditated upon; but for the sake of obtaining food for my own soul. The result I have found to be almost invariably this, that after a very few minutes my soul has been led to confession, or to thanksgiving, or to intercession, or to supplication; so that though I did not, as it were, give myself to prayer, but to meditation, yet it turned almost immediately more or less into prayer.

> When thus I have been for a while making confession, or intercession, or supplication, or have given thanks, I go on to the next words or verse, turning all, as I go on, into prayer for myself or others, as the Word may lead to it; but still continually keeping before me, that food for my own soul is the object of my meditation. The result of this is, that there is always a good deal of confession, thanksgiving, supplication, or intercession mingled with my meditation,

and that my inner man almost invariably is even sensi-
bly nourished and strengthened and that by breakfast time,
with rare exceptions, I am in a peaceful if not happy state
of heart...

By the blessing of God I ascribe to this mode the help
and strength which I have had from God to pass in peace
through deeper trials in various ways than I had ever had
before; and after having now above forty years tried this
way, I can most fully, in the fear of God, commend it. How
different when the soul is refreshed and made happy early
in the morning, from what is when, without spiritual prep-
aration, the service, the trials and the temptations of the
day come upon one![3]

Müller didn't just read his Bible, he prayed his Bible. Jesus wants you
to do the same. If you do, you'll never run out of prayer material.

DAILY REFLECTION

What are the main ways you struggle with the Vague Prayer
Syndrome? What do your vague prayers sound like? How could
they be made more specific?

_____

_____

What are three Bible passages from which you could start praying daily for yourself? For your work? Your family? Why did you
pick those?

_____

_____

If you're going through this with others, what are three to five Bible verses you could start praying collectively for some purpose?

DAILY PRAYER PROMPT

B—Believe God can do anything.

E—Embrace your childlike identity.

S—Specify your requests.

T—Trust God to do what's best with your requests.

DAILY PRAYER

God, help me pray with specificity. Give me the courage to be specific. Cause my Bible reading to be more prayerful. Protect me from being someone who just reads your Word without praying your Word. Ignite my holy imagination so that when I read passages, it naturally thinks of ways to pray the truths of that particular passage for my particular day. Help me to pray my Bible passages for those around me as well. Amen.

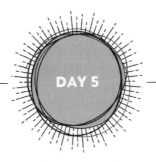

PRAY YOUR PLANS

The story of every great Christian achievement
is the history of answered prayer.

E.M. BOUNDS

Let the favor of the Lord our God be upon us,
and establish the work of our hands upon us;
yes, establish the work of our hands!

PSALM 90:17

R eady, Dad?" Judah asked. He had on his John Deere hat, some over-
sized work gloves, and a pair of boots. He was as ready to work as any
three-year-old could be. His older two siblings were already working to
make our gigantic flower beds, which were filled with everything but flowers, less embarrassing.

If you just listened to the way they worked, you'd think they were
accomplishing a ton. They sighed, took deep breaths, announced loudly
that they "needed to get some water," clanged their tools, and other things
you'd expect a top-notch work crew to do.

While their noises would have made you think that the work was moving forward efficiently, your eyes would have told another story. When I
looked at the work they'd done, I was pretty sure their current pace would
have them finishing the job just in time to graduate from high school.

I think they knew their output wasn't what it needed to be because pretty soon after they started working, they started asking, "Dad (or Mom), can you come help me with my part?" Why were they doing this? They recognized that parents increase productivity. We could do more in five minutes than they could probably do in five hours.

A similar reality is at play between our work and our Father's work, although the productivity gap is even greater between us and our heavenly Father. God can do more in a moment than we can do in a lifetime. The Bible is filled with examples of God's stunning strength. He creates everything out of nothing (Genesis 1). He splits the Red Sea, creating a path for the Israelite slaves to walk through on dry land (Exodus 14). He shut the mouths of lions so that Daniel could spend the night with them without one tooth mark on his skin (Daniel 6). He enabled Shadrach, Meshach, and Abednego to walk around in a massive fire without being harmed (Daniel 3). He brought Lazarus back from the dead (John 11). He made a way for Peter to walk out of a prison the night before he was supposed to be executed (Acts 12). God cannot be stopped.

But Jesus doesn't just want us to be aware of God's great power, he wants us to ask him to use his power to help us with our plans. He intends for us to be prayerfully productive. When we are prayerfully productive we are simply acting as my kids did in the front yard that day where they asked for parental help with their tasks. "God, will you come help me with my work?" God's children pray their plans.

That's one of the things Jesus is trying to help us see when he tells us to pray that our heavenly Father's "kingdom come, his will be done, on earth as it is in heaven." As we saw last chapter, part of praying this way means we pray our Bibles. But it means more. It means we pray our plans. Because the assumption underneath this prayer is that God's children are seeking "first the kingdom of God" (Matthew 6:33) in all that they do. That is, wherever they are, their plans are meant to advance God's purposes.

All of God's children are in the "family business." Every day is a "family workday." Whether you are paid or unpaid for your work, in the music business or the financial industry, you have work that God wants to help you with. You have been placed where you are by your heavenly Father to advance his heavenly purposes.

A lot of times we miss this aspect of Jesus' teaching on prayer because we have a secular view of the sacred. We have a small view of the kingdom and, therefore, of God's kingdom purposes. Many of us think that God wants us to ask him for help for "spiritual" things like going to church and reading our Bibles. And that's certainly true. God wants us to ask him to help us do those things.

But he's concerned about and wants to help with all of our lives. The apostle Paul points to God's concern for every area of life in 1 Corinthians 10:31, "So, whether you eat or drink, or whatever you do, do all to the glory of God."

"Whatever you do…" Paul says. That means God cares about everything you are doing today. Changing a kid's diapers? Have an important presentation? Trying to increase revenue? Working on email? Planning a vacation? The Bible says God cares about all of that. He wants us to glorify him in how we do that. The word *glorify* points to the same outcome we are asking for when we ask "your kingdom come, your will be done, on earth as it is in heaven."

Every day is a family workday for God's children. And he is interested in helping us with all of our lives. We show that we recognize this reality when we pray our plans.

Think about the first picture of "spiritual work" that God shows us in the Bible. It's a man and woman, Adam and Eve, working with their hands in a garden, naming animals, creating a family, and more. That hardly seems spiritual by today's standards, but it is by God's.

If they hadn't rejected God's perfect design in Genesis 3, they would have been perfectly, prayerfully productive. They would have asked for God's help every day to carry out the tasks God gave them. And they would have done it with specificity.

Do you pray your plans?

Many people don't. Many people think God doesn't care about their tasks and goals. They don't think God is willing to help them with their work, whether it is paid or unpaid. It's hard for them to imagine that God might really want to enable them to accomplish more than their competencies, their history, or their circumstances would seem to indicate was possible.

But when you really stop to think about that view of God, it's not one that looks anything like the God in the Bible. Even decent parents want to help their kids do well in all of their life. But we can only do so much.

The Bible says our heavenly Father is perfectly loving, unmatchably wise, endlessly knowledgeable, and overflowing with grace and mercy. After all, our heavenly Father loved us so much that he sent his Son to die in our place to secure a place for us in his family. If he did that, don't you think he cares more than the average parent? Isn't it possible that your view of his love is much too low and that it shows in your lack of prayer for your plans?

Jesus points us to a praying life that includes daily requests for help with our tasks. The world often simply points us to a new method that can help us become more productive. The Bible says we can become more productive by looking to the right God.

During one of the first prayer initiatives at the church I lead, where I challenged people to "pray their plans," a professor who had been working incredibly hard to get a book published took me up on the challenge. The author was as qualified as any author in his field, had a work ethic that outpaced most, and had several compelling book proposals that he'd sent to some publishing houses. He had great plans but no publishing contract. So he started to pray. He asked God to give him a book contract during the season of prayer that we were in. Amazingly, a publisher, whom he had not contacted, reached out to him about writing another book that he hadn't conceived of yet. He had the book contract he wanted, but in a way he never saw coming. When we pray our plans, our possibilities are endless.

Another family prayed their vacation plans. They were going to be in a region of the country they usually didn't visit because they were spending a few days with a part of their extended family they usually didn't get a chance to see. While they were there, they wanted to go to a nearby site they'd never seen. They'd always wanted to visit there, but they just couldn't afford to make it happen—even on this trip. So, they asked God to provide a free place. They didn't know how he would do it, but they knew that he could. And they asked that he'd do it in a week. Then, in a couple of days, they accidentally "pocket dialed" an old friend. As they were catching up, they talked about their upcoming plans. Unbelievably, the friend said he knew someone in that area who had a free place to stay and that he'd be willing to track it down. That week God provided a free place for their family to vacation in a city they'd always wanted to go to but were never able! When we pray our plans, our possibilities are endless.

I could give story after story of people praying their plans and God answering those plans, reports from the church world and the nonchurch world. Does he always answer our requests as we want him to? No. We'll talk more about that in just a couple of days. But it's important now to understand that he often does.

And he answers these requests for imperfect children who are making genuine but imperfect efforts to advance his kingdom purposes in their ordinary lives.

Pray your plans and you'll never run out of prayer material.

What does this look like practically?

I've found the most helpful approach for most people is to identify their "Top Six Roles," and then make prayer goals in each one. Taking a cue from the productivity genius, Stephen Covey, and his "roles to goals," every child of God should be able to easily identify their top six roles.

My top six roles right now are: Christian, Family, Pastor, Church Member, Friend, and Misc. In each of these roles, I have specific prayer requests that I'd like to see God answer each week and the time frame for his response. My work goals are on my prayer list. But there are, of course, goals that I'd rather not share with others.

Paul Miller, author of the life-changing prayer book *A Praying Life*, advises his readers to create note cards for these roles. You'll need to figure out your own approach. (I've found the Evernote app suits me best.)

But to get you started, we are going to spend some time today identifying your top six roles and what you'd like to see God do this week. My top six roles are:

Christian

- Cause me to love, enjoy, and be preoccupied with who you are more than with what I feel like you're calling me to do this week.

- Help me see ten answers to specific prayers this month.

Family

- Cause my kids to surrender their lives to you this month.
- Make this week with Melanie one of the best we have ever had.
- Provide a floor color that Melanie loves.

Pastor

- Cause the sermon to come together quickly and powerfully this week.
- Send an encouraging word to me from an unusual source today.
- Cause three people to surrender their lives to Jesus this month in our worship gatherings.
- Provide the finances for our budget this year.

Church Member

- Help me connect with others at my church this month.
- Cause my kids to grow in the kids' ministry in a way that seems unusually good this week.

Friend

- Help Bobby find a job by the end of the week.
- Cause the Osbornes's baby to get well without breathing treatments this week.
- Give Tony a raise this month.

Miscellaneous

- Provide a plumber for our renovation project this week who is kind, reasonable, and on time.
- Cause the workers to finish the work in a way that makes us more excited than we thought we'd be.

- Provide by Tuesday a vacation condo at an affordable price that we could all be excited about.

What are your roles? Individual, family, worker, friend, church member?

Once you've written down your prayer goals, then you are ready to pray your "Top Four Tasks" for the day. Sure, you have a lot of things to do each day in each role, but there are just a few, move-the-ball-forward tasks that you can do each day. I've found it helpful to identity and pray for specific outcomes for my top four tasks each day. These top four are usually found on the prayer goals list under my main six roles. I circle my top four to help me focus on those in particular. Perhaps that will help you as well.

DAILY REFLECTION

What are your six roles? What goals would you like God's help to bring about?

_____

_____

What goals are you already pursuing for which you need to start praying?

_____

_____

What goals do you need to add that you'd like to see happen but don't think you have the ability or time to bring about?

_____

_____

What are your top four tasks today? What would you like to see God do?

_____

_____

DAILY PRAYER PROMPT

B—Believe God can do anything.
E—Embrace your childlike identity.
S—Specify your requests.
T—Trust God to do what's best with your requests.

DAILY PRAYER

God, help me understand the six main roles through which you are calling me to advance your kingdom. Enable me to articulate what's on my heart, what has my attention, how I'd love to see you help me. Cause me to write specific requests, some of which seem possible without you and others that seem beyond my abilities. Please help me live a daily work life with your presence and power in view. Enable me to see you at work this week in my work. Amen.

Top Six Roles

Role 1: _____

What you'd like to see God do this week:

_____

Role 2: _____

What you'd like to see God do this week:

_____

*Role 3:*_____

What you'd like to see God do this week:

_____

*Role 4:*_____

What you'd like to see God do this week:

_____

*Role 5:*_____

What you'd like to see God do this week:

_____

*Role 6:*_____

What you'd like to see God do this week

_____

Top Four Tasks

1._____

2._____

3._____

4._____

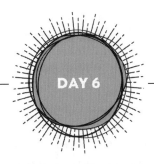

DAY 6

PRAY YOUR PROBLEMS

In studying the psalms we get a pretty good idea of what prayer is. It is talking to God; telling him all about ourselves, our cares, our anxieties, our troubles, vexations, disappointments, in a word, unbosoming ourselves to him as we would to a confidential friend.

FRANCIS GRIMKÉ

Be not far from me,
for trouble is near,
and there is none to help.

PSALM 22:11

Parents have to teach their kids a lot of things. They have to teach them how to eat, how to use a toilet, how to comb their hair, and so on.

But parents don't have to teach their kids how to let them know they have a problem they need help with. As soon as babies are born, they let us know when they are unhappy. They cry and they cry. They don't know how to speak, but they know how to communicate.

Jesus wants his followers, those who have been born again, to communicate with their heavenly Father about their problems as well. That's why every request in the Lord's Prayer starts with some kind of problem. We say, "Hallowed be your name," because his name isn't being hallowed as it should—which is a problem from heaven's perspective. We request, "Your kingdom come, your will be done," because his kingdom does not seem to be here, and his will isn't really being done. That's a problem. Then there's a provision problem that leads to us ask, "Give us this day our daily bread." And then a guilt problem that causes us to plead "and forgive us our debts." And because we have a problem with evil, we ask God to "deliver us from evil."

This isn't, of course, the only place where problems are prayed. When Israel was enslaved in Egypt, they prayed their problem. They "cried out to God." When Hannah was burdened by her childlessness, she prayed her problem with tears (1 Samuel 1). When Nehemiah heard that the walls in Jerusalem were broken, he cried out to God in prayer (Nehemiah 1). When Peter was one day away from being executed by Rome, the church prayed him out of prison (Acts 12).

The book of Psalms is filled with examples of people praying their problems. In Psalm 69, the writer pleads, "Save me God, the water has risen to my neck." The writer of Psalm 5 is so overwhelmed by his problems he can't find the words, so he says, "Consider my sighing and I'll watch expectantly." Psalm 51 is based on a guilt problem where the author is looking for grace. In Psalm 22, the writer feels forsaken. In Psalm 55, the writer feels betrayed by a friend. The Bible shows people praying their problems over and over.

Thankfully, Jesus says, "Come to me, all of you who are weary and burdened..." (Matthew 11:28 CSB). What makes you "weary" and "burdened"? Problems.

Do you pray your problems?

Most people don't. Most people initially either try to run away from their problems or run to their problems—flight or fight. Those that run away from difficulty usually try to escape to some other, safer world. Whether that other world is online, at the gym, with comfort food, or in a bottle, it never solves problems and sometimes creates new ones.

Those who run to the problem in their own strength typically just overwork, get angry, burn out, or burn things down. Sure, they can handle more problems than most, but everybody eventually runs into more problems than they can handle on their own.

Jesus doesn't want you to run away from or to your problems. He wants you to run to the Father with your problems. When you learn to pray your problems, you learn the secret to praying "without ceasing" (1 Thessalonians 5:17). Your prayers are unceasing because your problems are unceasing. Whether your prayers seem little or big, God wants his children to bring every one of them to him. Because each specific problem prayed gives the invisible God an opportunity to become visible in the prayer's life. So turn your problems into prayers.

What problems do you need to pray?

Here's an awesome truth. When you pray your problems, you turn your problems into platforms. What's that mean? It means that when you ask God to do something about a specific problem (such as asking him to solve a financial, health, relational, or professional problem), you turn that problem into a platform where you can see something of God that you couldn't without that problem.

That's what the apostle Paul is explaining to the Corinthian Christians in 2 Corinthians 12. After saying that he asked God to remove a problem, one that he called "a thorn in the flesh," God told him, "My grace is sufficient for you, for my power is made perfect in weakness" (12:9). Paul points God to his problem and God points Paul to an experience of his grace and power. Where is God's power, something everyone wants to experience? It's experienced most in our weakness, in our problems. Problems are platforms.

This truth is the reason why Paul goes on to let the Corinthian Christians know that he actually looks forward to the next problem because he knows that when God is brought into our problems through prayer, problems turn into platforms that enable us to see and experience God in a way that we wouldn't without those problems. He says, "For the sake of Christ, then, I am content with weaknesses, insults, hardships, persecutions, and calamities. For when I am weak, then I am strong" (12:10). He is "content with" or "delights in" what? Weaknesses, insults, hardships, persecutions, and calamities. I'm not sure what's on your list of "things I like to avoid," but my guess is that things like these are on it.

Why does Paul feel so differently about his problems? Because he sees something we don't see. He understands problems can become platforms when we pray our problems. This changes how we view our difficulties. We see that God uses our problems to prepare us.

Paul, of course, didn't look forward to every aspect of those problems. He wasn't crazy, although he sounded a bit like it in this passage. Earlier in this letter to the Corinthian Christians he let them know that he'd been tortured for Christ and that there were times when he and his companions were "so utterly burdened beyond our strength that we despaired of life itself. Indeed, we felt that we had received the sentence of death. But that was to make us rely not on ourselves but on God who raises the dead" (2 Corinthians 1:8-9). Did you see it? There were parts of the problem that he hated. Those parts made him "despair of life itself." But, he says, in that awful experience, God was extending grace that enabled him to grow—learning how to rely even more heavily on the God who "raises the dead."

Paul prayed his problems and it turned his problems into platforms. Do you do the same?

Over the course of the last several years, we've seen hundreds of answers to problems. One of my favorites came from a guy who was always an overachiever. Whether climbing the ranks on the baseball field to the major leagues, teaching himself to play the guitar for fun, or mastering just about any board game you put in front of him, his competitive drive and unique gifting made him stand out in just about every crowd.

That's what made the work situation he was telling me about so frustrating. For six years, he had excelled. Because of his great performance, he was given more responsibility. Unfortunately, while his workload grew significantly, his pay didn't at all. Hesitant to confront, he just kept his head down, continued to grind, and hoped for a different future.

We had no idea that he was struggling with this problem when we launched a season of specific prayer at our church. His small group didn't either. But right after I introduced this idea of praying your problems, he told them about his work situation and that he was going to start "praying his problem."

That was a Sunday. The very next day, his boss asked to meet with him. It was an unusual request and it scared him to death. In fact, he called me that night, worried that he might be losing his job.

After hearing about his situation and his prayer, I asked him if he thought God might be answering his prayer? "Maybe so," he said. But it certainly wasn't the first thought that jumped into his head. So, I prayed for him, and then asked him to follow up with me.

He met with his boss that Wednesday and it went great. He got that raise he was praying for! He was so excited to tell us about it.

Because my friend prayed his problems, God turned his problem into a platform—a place where he and his Christian friends got to experience God's power and love in a dramatic way. Because of that experience, the problem and the answer to prayer, his childlike faith in his heavenly Father deepened, igniting joy, excitement, hope, and peace in his heart. You had better believe that going forward he was asking God to do more with his problems and plans through prayer.

Does God always answer our prayers the way we want? Again, no. But most of us don't have trouble believing that. People typically have more trouble believing that he answers any specific prayers like that.

I don't know your story, but I know you have problems. Everyone has them. For some, they are financial difficulties; others are troubled by relational tensions or the loss of health. Career difficulties usually appear at the top of the list. And, of course, there are the small, everyday annoyances. No one chooses these problems, but they seem to choose us. Whatever the problems you face, God has a unique plan for you. Part of that plan includes your praying your problems so that they turn into platforms for you and others to see God's power, love, and wisdom in your life.

I'll never forget how God turned one of my problems into a platform in January 2019. In December 2018, I prayed for a record-high giving month for our church. We had the largest staff that we had had in quite a long time. I was anxious that our young church plant wouldn't be able to meet all our financial obligations. So I prayed that God would give us a financial cushion that would give us confidence that he would provide for us moving forward.

Much to my surprise, we had the lowest December giving amount that we had had since our church started! As anyone involved in leading a ministry knows, December giving often saves the annual budget. Having just taken on some significant new costs—adding staff and moving into a new building—this record low was especially concerning. We were about $90,000 under what I was praying for, which was a massive amount for our small church.

But that next month, we were having a 21 Days of Prayer initiative. In it, I asked, as was my practice, that everyone would pray for specific things as I did every time. You'd better believe that I was praying that God would make up the financial loss, although I didn't know how, humanly speaking, that would happen.

Out of the blue, someone in our church, who wasn't even a member, asked me to go to breakfast. Over that breakfast, he told me that he'd just gotten a massive raise and that he would be increasing his giving to the church. And that amount would equal, over the course of the year, the difference between what we got in December and what I was praying for. Amazing!

As you can imagine, I left that breakfast floating on air I was so happy.

I don't know all the reasons for that December no, but I sense one of them has to be that God didn't want me looking to a big month to provide for my needs; he wanted me looking to him—a big God who provides for his kids.

DAILY REFLECTION

What problems are weighing on you today?

When problems come into your life do you have "fight" or "flight" tendencies? Why do you think that is? How have you seen these tendencies make things worse, not better?

If God promised to solve your three biggest problems, what would those be? What would you want him to do? Start praying those.

Take a few moments to write down exactly what you would like God to do to help with the top three problems in your life.

DAILY PRAYER PROMPT

B—Believe God can do anything.

E—Embrace your childlike identity.

S—Specify your requests.

T—Trust God to do what's best with your requests.

DAILY PRAYER

God, please increase my awareness of the major problems that are weighing on me. Enable me to come up with specific outcomes for them. Cause big and small problems to end up on my prayer list today and that some would be answered this week. Amen.

What specific requests do you need to make for the roles God's given you today?

Role 1: _____

What you'd like to see God do this week:

_____

Role 2: _____

What you'd like to see God do this week:

_____

Role 3: _____

What you'd like to see God do this week:

_____

Role 4: _____

What you'd like to see God do this week:

_____

Role 5: _____

What you'd like to see God do this week:

_____

Role 6: _____

What you'd like to see God do this week:

_____

Top Four Tasks

1. _____

2. _____

3. _____

4. _____

Trust God to Do What's Best with Your Requests

*God will either give us what we ask or give us what we
would have asked if we knew everything he knows.*

Tim Keller

*Some trust in chariots and some in horses,
but we trust in the name of the Lord our God.*

Psalm 20:7

"O uch! I'm telling!" Judah, my youngest son, complained.
As expected, immediately, I heard him making his way to me
in the kitchen, where I was going through the mail. With tears just about
to run down his cheeks, Judah told me all about the great injustice he
endured.

I had just returned home from work and was a bit tired. So, I said to
him, "I'll take care of it." With that, his countenance changed, and he
joyfully walked right back where he'd come from. I overheard him self-
righteously say to his sibling, "Dad said he'll take care of it."

He didn't know *how* or even *when* I would take care of it. Frankly, he
didn't know if I would take care of it at all. He simply knew *who* would
take care of it. Because he knew who would take care of his problem, he
walked out of that conversation without the burden he brought into it.

That burden-relieving, peace-producing, change-you-right-where-you-are-from-the-inside-out kind of interaction happens only when there is an unshakable trust in the one to whom you just presented your problem. That's childlike trust.

Our interactions with God are supposed to happen that way. That's what it looks like to "cast your burden on the LORD" (Psalm 55:22; 1 Peter 5:7). In prayer, our childlike faith leads us to the Father with our burden, and our childlike trust enables us to leave the conversation without it. Childlike trust is wrapped up in the "your will be done" part of the Lord's Prayer. Our prayers are requests for what we think are best. Childlike trust says, "I trust you to do what is best with my request."

Remember, Jesus says we are talking with the God of the heavens who created all things, sustains all things, works his mysterious, sovereign will for the good of those who love him, raises up kingdoms, flattens kingdoms, raised the dead, defeated death, healed the sick, gave sight to the blind, enabled men to survive Babylon's flames, shut the mouths of lions, just to name a few things. Not a bad resume! He knows all things, loves perfectly, and is incredibly gracious. While we can know him truly, we'll never know him completely. He is an amazing God!

Sometimes we forget the One to whom we are talking. Oftentimes, somewhere in our conversation with the great and gracious God, we start to feel like we know what's best for us, regardless of the situation. That's why it is so important to remember who God is. If God is great enough to answer your prayers and those of everyone else praying to him, he is great enough to have a better way that you don't understand.

Childlike trust rests on the power, love, and wisdom of God. Because he is all-powerful, I don't have to worry about something stopping him from doing what is best for me. Because he loves his children with an unending love, I can be assured that he will always do what's best for me. Because he's all-wise, I know he always takes the best way. Childlike trust rests in his revealed character, not in the knowledge of his secret plans.

That's why it is so important to think about the words that we often use to end our prayers—"in Jesus' name." We don't say this because we have to. Jesus didn't end his prayer in Matthew 6 in that way. He said at the beginning of his now famous prayer to pray "like" this (Matthew 6:9). His teaching wasn't primarily concerned with the order of the wording, but with the elements of the prayer. Yet we do this because, in other passages, he talks to his disciples about asking "in his name" (John 14).

It is important that we pray "in Jesus' name." We should not treat his name like a secret password. Instead, we should be reminded of the powerful gospel truth that we can come to God "in Jesus' name" because of Jesus' death in our place on the cross. Because of the cross, we should never question his love. Because of the empty tomb, we should never question his power. And because of the whole plan, we should never question his wisdom. No one thought that anything good could come from Jesus' death on the day of his death. Little did anyone know that Jesus would make the seemingly worst day into the best day with the best news ever.

Do you trust God like a child? Do you trust him enough to be thankful for his *no*s to your requests because you know that every no is a yes to something better?

When you do, you've learned the secret to experiencing a deep inner peace in the midst of incredibly difficult circumstances. That inner peace doesn't just change your daily life; it has a powerful impact on the world around you—an impact we all desperately need.

I love how Paul Miller puts this reality: "Learning to pray doesn't offer us a less busy life; it offers us a less busy heart."[4]

How does the praying life offer us a less busy heart? When we trust God to do what's best with our request. When we offer up our request with the heart belief that "God will either give us what we ask or give us what we would have asked if we knew everything he knows."[5]

Childlike trust doesn't pretend that difficult things don't exist, it gives you the courage to face them without flinching. It helps us wake up every day and, without fearful hearts, pursue goals that we feel are impossible for us to bring about. When we trust God, we can face the worst-case-scenario possibilities that run through our heads and hearts at work and at home.

Recently, some friends of mine were battling to have a heart of childlike trust as they got ready to take their five-month-old, nonstop-smiling son to the doctor. Their son had a little skin tag on the back of his head that needed to be removed, and they were anxious that he might need to be put under in order to remove it.

After sitting in their room at the doctor's office for a while, they began to grow even more worried. Eventually, the doctor broke to them the terrifying news. As they had examined their son's skin tag, they'd discovered that his skull wasn't pieced together properly for it to expand as he grew. His only chance for future health was to undergo a significant operation on his skull.

My friends were devastated. As they lined up the details for the surgery, they began to pray this problem. Quickly, they invited the rest of our church and others to plead with God on their son's behalf.

With less than a week away, the child's mom spoke about their perspective on their son's upcoming surgery. She said that they, and everyone they knew, were praying for him, that they trusted God to do what was best with him: "If God takes him, it would be our greatest nightmare. But we're at peace with whatever God wants." There wasn't a dry eye in the room.

They didn't know God's plan, but they knew God's character. Because they knew the One to whom they were talking, they were able to walk through one of those "worst-case-scenario" situations that we all find ourselves in at some point, with the peace "which surpasses all understanding" (Philippians 4:6-7). That's what childlike trust looks like.

Their son came out of the surgery just fine. He has a massive scar on his head from the surgery, but that doesn't keep him from lighting up every room he's in with his world-class smile.

My friends have new burdens that they are trying to "cast on the Lord," and so do you. If you're going through this with a group, you probably have some collective "worst case scenarios." If you want to experience the freedom and peace that God offers in the midst of your trials, remember to trust him to do what is best with your request. When you don't know God's plan, meditate on God's character, and you'll be able to walk fearlessly into horrifying circumstances.

Is your heart marked by a childlike trust?

It won't be easy. Most of my prayer requests have not been answered in ways I thought were best. And while it might be easy to think that God doesn't answer prayers anymore, that my sincere request offered from a heart of faith needed more faith, or some other missing ingredient, the Bible points us back to a heavenly Father who always does what's best for his children. Because of the cross, we should never question his love. Because of the empty tomb, we should never question his power. Because of the unexpected way that Jesus provided salvation, we should never question his wisdom.

God wants you to think about *nos* to your prayer requests, not as a problem with your faith, but a problem with your perspective. If you could see everything that he sees, you'd answer prayers as he answers them.

The apostle Paul tells us that we have a Father "who is able to do above and beyond all that we ask or think" (Ephesians 3:20 csb). That means God has purposes for your good that you can't understand. Paul wants to help us remember the God who does "above and beyond all that we ask or think" if we get the cancer diagnosis, if our spouse won't come back, if our kid doesn't make the team, or if a friendship doesn't seem salvageable.

I'll never forget a season in our church that lasted for a couple of years. It was the hardest time in my life. It was hard to get out of bed. I felt like I lived in a constant fog. There was a transition at church that led to a relational disaster. It was a perfect storm.

Close friends walked away, things were said that I felt were untrue and unfair, giving went down significantly, just to name a few things. I made mistakes. Others made mistakes. It was a tough season made worse by my lack of trust in God.

And in the midst of that season, I prayed and prayed that God would fix tons of specific problems. I prayed for wisdom. I prayed through tears. I prayed my fears. And just about everything I asked God to do, he didn't do.

There is much I don't understand about why God allowed that to happen. I know he used it to teach me to pray. Many of the ways that I'm most useful to people I learned through that difficult time.

But here I am. I have the choice, either to believe that God doesn't let anything happen to me that isn't ultimately best for me, or to go with my understanding that says, "He blew it back there." One of those options involves trust in him and the other doesn't. The one with trust brings peace and the other cynicism.

The book of Job shows us that God doesn't always do what we think is best. The book of Job starts with Job losing just about everything. Most of the book is Job agonizing in prayer before God. He doesn't think he can live the life God is calling him to live.

Then, "out of the whirlwind," the Lord answers Job by pointing him to his character as Creator and Sustainer of the world (Job 38:1). In Job 42, Job prays a prayer of repentance and worship. His heart is changed in this fresh vision of God in prayer.

As Tim Keller says, meditating on this passage, "The more clearly Job saw who God was, the fuller his prayers became—moving from mere complaint to confession, appeal, and praise. In the end he broke through and was able to face anything in life."[6]

I don't want what happened to Job to happen to you, but I do want you to have Job's childlike trust that helped him endure and move past incredible difficulty.

As you struggle to trust your heavenly Father, remember that Jesus didn't always get a yes. In the Garden of Gethsemane, Jesus asked three times that the cup of God's wrath would be removed from him. But because it wasn't best for us, the cup wasn't removed. So Jesus said, "Not my will, but yours be done." Jesus was told no in the Garden of Gethsemane so that he could tell us yes to our request for salvation in our sin. Jesus drank the cup of God's wrath so that he could enable us to drink the cup of God's mercy.

Next time you are struggling to trust God in a way that enables you to walk out of your prayer time with him without the burden you brought into it, reflect on God's no to Jesus in the Garden of Gethsemane. Perhaps, as in Jesus' situation, the no won't make sense to us until after the resurrection. Trust him now, while we wait for that day. Remember that no one can take anything away from us that God thinks is best for us.

One daily discipline that can help foster this childlike trust in your heart is thanking God for at least three things to start your day. These can be things that you're excited about or things that you aren't. Why would you thank God for things that you might not be happy about? Because you are reminding yourself that God always does what's best for his kids.

DAILY REFLECTION

Childlike trust depends on a specific view of God's love, wisdom, and power. Which of these three characteristics do you find it easiest and most difficult to believe in? Why?

_____

_____

What are the top three areas in your life that you are struggling to trust God with right now? Why?

_____

_____

_____

If you are going through this with a group, what are the most difficult areas to trust God collectively?

_____

_____

Take a few moments to write down exactly what you fear might happen with your top three problems and that you trust God to do what's best with your request. Then ask God to give you the childlike trust that enables you to be at peace while you wait on his answer.

DAILY PRAYER PROMPT

B—Believe God can do anything.
E—Embrace your childlike identity.
S—Specify your requests.
T—Trust God to do what's best with your requests.

DAILY PRAYER

God, cause my heart to trust you. Enable me to identify and specify requests that I have for you. Help me to cast my burden on you and to walk away freely. Cause it to be said of my heart what was said of the man the psalmist described, "He will not fear bad news; his heart is confident, trusting in the LORD. His heart is assured; he will not fear" (Psalm 112:7-8 CSB). Thank you for doing what's best for me. Amen.

Because God always does what's best for his children, what are three things you can thank him for today?

What specific requests do you need to make for the roles God's given you today?

Role 1: _____

What you'd like to see God do this week:

_____

Role 2: _____

What you'd like to see God do this week:

_____

Role 3: _____

What you'd like to see God do this week:

_____

Role 4: _____

What you'd like to see God do this week:

_____

*Role 5:*_____

What you'd like to see God do this week:

_____

*Role 6:*_____

What you'd like to see God do this week:

_____

Top Four Tasks

1._____

2._____

3._____

4._____

Top Three Thank-Yous

1._____

2._____

3._____

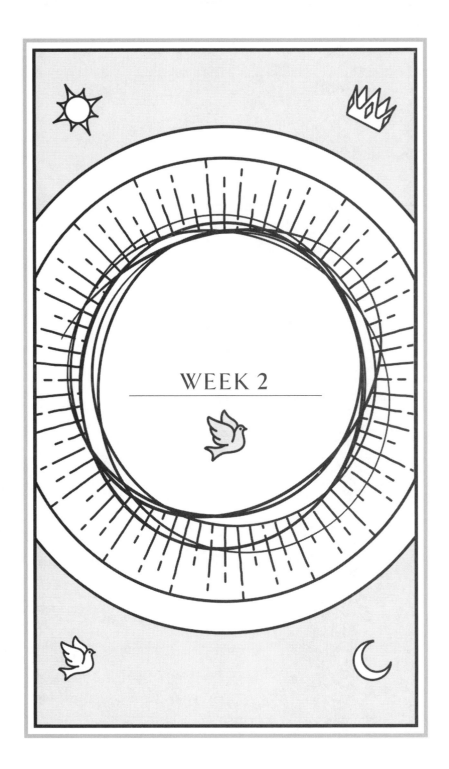

WEEK 2

DAY 8

Six Childlike Prayer Practices

Things happen which would not happen
without prayer. Let us not forget that.

ELISABETH ELLIOT

Turn to me and be gracious to me,
for I am lonely and afflicted.
The troubles of my heart are enlarged;
bring me out of my distresses.

PSALM 25:16-17

Over the past week, you learned about the Four Foundational Child-like Prayer Principles:

B—Believe God can do anything.

E—Embrace your childlike identity.

S—Specify your requests.

T—Trust God to do what's best with your requests.

In order to have a daily prayer life, we need to see God for who he is. When we do that, we believe that God can do anything. If we don't believe this, we won't pray. It's that simple.

A childlike prayer life continues when we embrace our childlike identity. Children are dependent on and bold toward their parents. We are encouraged to have that same boldness when we think about our prayer life. If we don't think we need God's help, we won't pray. Jesus teaches us to pray in a way that reminds us of our childlike identity.

A childlike prayer life flourishes when we specify our requests like a child. Children get specific in a way most adults don't. When we get specific, we give the invisible God a way to become visible in our lives. Specificity leads to visibility. This means we have to battle "Vague Prayer Syndrome." And we can get specific in three primary ways: praying our Bible passages, praying our problems, and praying our plans.

A childlike prayer life peacefully ends when, like a child, we trust God to do what's best with our requests. If we have a God big enough to answer all of our prayers, we have a God who is big enough to have good reasons for answering our prayers not the way we want but in a way that is best for us.

Now that we've introduced the Four Foundational Childlike Prayer Principles, we are ready to move on to the Six Childlike Prayer Practices. These practices are critical to fostering the daily childlike characteristics Jesus intends for us to have.

As the number of tasks at the end of each day's reading has increased, it's important to remember that you don't need to do every one of them every day. Do the one(s) that are most helpful for you and/or the group.

DAILY REFLECTION

What are your prayer goals for this week?

_____

_____

What part was most challenging to you in week one? Why?

_____

_____

What part was most helpful to you in week one? Why?

_____

_____

What specific requests do you need to make for the roles God's given you today?

_____

_____

Role 1: _____

What you'd like to see God do this week:

_____

Role 2: _____

What you'd like to see God do this week:

_____

Role 3: _____

What you'd like to see God do this week:

_____

Role 4: _____

What you'd like to see God do this week:

_____

Role 5: _____

What you'd like to see God do this week:

_____

Role 6: _____

What you'd like to see God do this week:

_____

Top Four Tasks

1. _____

2. _____

3. _____

4. _____

Top Three Thank-Yous

1. _____

2. _____

3. _____

DAY 9

PRIORITIZING A PRIVATE PRAYER TIME

Prayer does not fit us for the greater work, prayer is the greater work.

OSWALD CHAMBERS

*And rising very early in the morning, while it was still dark, he
departed and went out to a desolate place, and there he prayed.*

MARK 1:35

Children need one-on-one time with their parents. Whether it is snuggling on the couch, watching a movie, going to grab some ice cream, or something else, children grow best when they have personal, away-from-everyone-else time with their parents. Every child psychologist, no matter their background or approach, agrees on this.

The same is true for God's children. Our relationship will grow the most with our heavenly Father when we prioritize a personal time with him. Thankfully, our heavenly Father is never too busy to meet with us. There will never be a time when God's children don't have their heavenly Father's undivided, totally engaged attention. We never have to say, "Dad, will you stop checking your phone." We'll never hear, "Maybe later, son." Our heavenly Father is so amazing that all of him, not some of him, is always available to all of his children.

The question is, will we make time for him?

Those listening to Jesus' teaching on prayer struggled to do this as well—and they didn't even have smartphone notifications pinging them! That's why Jesus told them in Matthew 6:5-6, which is right before the prayer that we looked at last week, that their heavenly Father prioritizes personal encounters. Jesus said,

> "When you pray, you must not be like the hypocrites. For they love to stand and pray in the synagogues and at the street corners, that they may be seen by others. Truly, I say to you, they have received their reward. But when you pray, go into your room and shut the door and pray to your Father who is in secret. And your Father who sees in secret will reward you."

Jesus says that their heavenly Father is interested in meeting and rewarding them privately. In a world that values public performances, even religious prayerful ones, Jesus wants his followers to know that private encounters with God in prayer should be a priority.

Do you have a personal time with your heavenly Father?

Thankfully, Jesus doesn't just tell us to prioritize a private time of prayer with our heavenly Father, he also models this approach for us. Jesus taught his disciples *what* to pray in Matthew 6, but he showed them *how* to pray throughout his ministry.

The Gospel of Mark tells us that Jesus rose early in the morning to pray in a desolate place early in his ministry. Jesus prayed after he fed the crowds (Mark 6:46). He prayed alone before he chose the Twelve (Luke 6:12-13). The Gospel of Luke tells us that before Peter confessed Jesus as the Christ, Jesus prayed alone (Luke 9:18-20). Right before the transfiguration, Jesus prayed alone (Luke 9:28). Also, Jesus prayed alone before his disciples asked him to teach them to pray (Luke 11:1). Before Jesus' crucifixion, he went alone to pray in the Garden of Gethsemane (Matthew 26:36-46; Mark 14:32-42; Luke 22:39-46).

Jesus prioritized a private prayer time.

Are you ready to make this a priority in your daily life?

Think about all the amazing things Jesus did in his life. He healed the blind, fed tens of thousands of people by miraculously multiplying a few pieces of food, raised a man named Lazarus from the dead, calmed the winds and the waves from a small boat in the Sea of Galilee, cast out demons, turned water into wine, just to name a few of Jesus' incredible achievements.

But what we often fail to see in Jesus' powerful ministry is the connection to his personal prayer time. Out of all the things God could have had written down about Jesus' ministry, he made sure that we saw Jesus' prayer life and his powerful acts. Why? He wants us to see the connection between them. He wants us to follow that pattern.

Before God uses us publicly, he wants to meet with us privately. The power of God displayed publicly in Jesus' ministry flows to a significant degree through Jesus' private prayer life.

Prioritizing a private prayer time, of course, isn't unique to Jesus' ministry. Daniel was a man who did the same. That's right, the famous Daniel and the lions' den.

Daniel lived in exile under Babylonian oppression. He lived out his faith in ways that eventually got him sentenced to death. And that death sentence was cruel and unusual. He was told that he would be thrown into a lions' den! But even though Daniel was thrown into that horrible, nasty-smelling den, he wasn't touched by the lions. He survived!

What people often miss about Daniel's story of deliverance is the way that Daniel prioritized private prayer time before that moment. The book of Daniel doesn't tell us a lot about Daniel's fascinating life, but it does tell us that he regularly prayed privately. Why might God want us to see that? Because God wants us to know that he wants to hear from us privately before he uses us powerfully.

And it wasn't just true for him. Moses prayed alone and was used powerfully. David prayed alone and did amazing things. Nehemiah was a man of action who pulled off one of the greatest leadership achievements in the world with the rebuilding of Jerusalem's walls. The list could go on and on.

Why does the Bible emphasize private prayer so much? Because it wants to make it clear that God is interested in a personal relationship with you. And every personal relationship, at least the most significant ones, have one-on-one time.

Many people, for whatever reason, have never prioritized a daily prayer time with God. Thankfully, anybody can do it, with God's help. I've found that the following four steps help people follow Jesus' teaching and example of making prayer a daily, meaningful reality in their life.

Identify your spot—Find a place where the chances of being uninterrupted are as high as they possibly can be. Right now, I go to my study and my wife goes to the living room couch. Figure out a spot that works for you. Identify your spot and you increase the chances that you'll pray every day.

Identify your time—Identify the right time for you. For some people, the morning is the best time, others the evening, still others sometime during the day. The key is to find a time that works for you. Not sure where to start? I encourage people to do what I do—I make time to start the day in prayer because I don't want to start the day without God's presence and promises in view.

Plan your time—A little planning will make a big impact. To plan your time, just identify what part of the Bible you want to read and pray, grab something to write with and on, and anything else you might want to have during that time (such as coffee!).

Prepare for resistance—The enemy hates for God's children to spend time with their heavenly Father. He hates for God to reward his children with his satisfying presence and specific answers to prayer. That's why no matter when you choose to do these things, get ready for random interruptions. I call it "the resistance." A kid will come in. Text messages will appear. Something good or bad will happen. It's always something. Prepare for resistance.

Did you hope to have forty-five minutes, but now you only have five minutes? That's okay—five minutes is better than zero minutes! Did you miss a morning? That's okay! Find time during the day to encounter God personally. Did you miss a day or a week? Don't let the enemy discourage you enough to make you quit. Your heavenly Father has enough blood-bought grace to get you started fresh today.

The Bible is filled with examples of people who prioritized private time with their heavenly Father before they were used powerfully publicly. What might God want to do in your life and ministry if you focused more on being with him in private prayer than working for him in public life and ministry?

DAILY REFLECTION

What's your spot? _____

What's your time? _____

What's your time going to look like?_____

What's your resistance to carrying this out look like? _____

_____

DAILY PRAYER PROMPT

B—Believe God can do anything.
E—Embrace your childlike identity.
S—Specify your requests.
T—Trust God to do what's best with your requests.

DAILY PRAYER

Father, help me prioritize a private prayer time with you. Cause it to be something that I look forward to. Enable me to know how best to prioritize it during the season of life that I'm in. Help me to say no to less important things that have less resistance and to say yes to this most important thing. Enable me to overcome the resistance that stands between a daily personal prayer time with you. Amen.

What specific requests do you need to make for the roles God's given you today?

Role 1: _____

What you'd like to see God do this week:

_____

Role 2: _____

What you'd like to see God do this week:

_____

Role 3: _____

What you'd like to see God do this week:

_____

Role 4: _____

What you'd like to see God do this week:

_____

Role 5: _____

What you'd like to see God do this week:

_____

Role 6: _____

What you'd like to see God do this week:

_____

Top Four Tasks

1. _____

2. _____

3. _____

4. _____

Top Three Thank-Yous

1. _____

2. _____

3. _____

DAY 10

THE SURPRISING POWER
OF WRITTEN PRAYERS

If a man write little, he hath need of a great memory.

FRANCIS BACON

They forgot his works and the wonders that he had shown them.

PSALM 78:11

Children don't recognize most of the tasks their parents do for them. They have no clue all of the work that is happening to make life work for them. Not until they have their own kids do they really appreciate what their parents did for them. I know that was certainly true for me.

But parents don't wait until their kids grow up and have their own kids to try to teach them to recognize and appreciate their parents' work. Parents spend tons of energy trying to do this. Why? Not primarily because thank-yous from children are that satisfying. Parents teach their kids to appreciate their work because parents want their kids to be in touch with reality.

Parents don't want their kids growing up thinking that dishes just get cleaned on their own, clothes washed and folded miraculously, food appears in the fridge, vacations are automatic, money grows on trees, and all the rest. But this is hard work because kids are born with the ability to ignore all the good their parents have done and to focus on what they still want done.

Sadly, all of us tend to do the same thing with our heavenly father. Like Adam and Eve, we tend to focus on the one thing at the moment that we want but God hasn't given us—ignoring all that he has provided. We aren't able to list off ways that our heavenly Father has answered specific prayers as quickly as we can talk about the ways we think God has failed us. And because of this tendency, we fail, like the children in our homes, to see reality as it truly is.

That's why it's so important to learn to consistently write down specific prayer requests and how they are answered. That's right, we're talking about journaling.

Now listen, I hate journaling. I wish I didn't, but I do. I'm the worst. I'm not sure if it's because I think it isn't fun enough, if it isn't productive enough, or what. But I stink at it.

I hate journaling, but I love encountering God's grace in a way that fosters childlike faith in a God who can do anything. I love seeing visible demonstrations that God cares about me personally and has shown up time and time again in my life. I count it a good day when I make my way through it with the kind of confidence in God that David had when he stepped onto the field to face Goliath with just a slingshot.

There are so many things I realized that I love that I can only get consistently if I journal consistently. As I'll show you in a just a few moments, not all journaling is as sophisticated as that word makes it sound.

When you plan your private prayer time with God, you need to include "writing specific prayer requests" and "answers"—whether those answers are yes or no. Why? Because when God pours out his grace through a specific answer to prayer, he doesn't just want to build up your childlike faith in that moment, he wants to build your childlike faith in the days ahead. He's providing spiritual food that can be used to feed your heart tomorrow. Written prayers help God's children remember God's gracious presence.

If you've ever read through the Bible, you've probably noticed that God commands his people to "remember" his works over and over. And the reason why God gives this command is that we tend to forget what God wants us to remember. Our forgetfulness is problematic because in large part, our remembering shapes the way we see our reality.

Chances are that you've seen an aging family member struggle to remember loved ones. Because of this loss of memory, the person doesn't know how to treat their loved ones. They have forgotten where they've been, so they struggle to know where the relationship should go.

Sadly, oftentimes we act the same way toward our God. We've forgotten where we've been with him, so we struggle to know where he'd like the relationship to go. We don't face our day from the perspective that Jesus won for us—seated at the right hand of God with all of God's resources, love, and strength in view. Because of our spiritual amnesia, we don't realize we're already at the top of the ladder, so there's no need to try to climb it today.

That's why figuring out your approach to prayer journaling is so important.

God loves for his works to be written down and thought about. He doesn't want his great works to impact people just on the day they happened, he wants them to be life giving throughout the ages.

But God doesn't want you to think that he stopped answering his children's prayers. He's inviting you to start capturing specific requests and answers to prayer so that you can join the psalmist who said,

> I will remember the deeds of the LORD;
>   yes, I will remember your wonders of old.
> I will ponder all your work,
>   and meditate on your mighty deeds
> (Psalm 77:11-12).

Are you already keeping a journal? Great! Keep it up! But if you aren't, here are five suggestions that have helped.

Find your journal—Some of you will prefer a traditional journal that's beautiful; others of you might use prayer cards. Or perhaps you'll be like me and use Evernote cards. Maybe you'll use several different things. That's okay. Find what works for you.

Find your writing style—The Bible has a lot of different writing styles. What's yours? Some of you write in a way that if it is discovered, people will be inspired by it. Others of you are like me and write in bullet points. One way you can do this is to write down sentences about how you feel and what you want God to do about it. Another way is for you just to write out bullet points with short sentences or sentence fragments and the date you want God to complete it by. You're not writing for an English teacher who is going to grade you. You're writing to remember.

Determine your privacy setting—Some people are okay with others reading their prayer requests, while others are not. If you aren't, I'd find a place to keep your journal private and let those around you know that you'd like it to stay private. Everybody needs a place to pour out their hearts to God.

Determine your prayer review schedule—One of the main ways you can build your childlike faith is by consistently reviewing the works of God. Whether it is once a month, once a week, once a quarter, or once a year, make sure that you look over your prayer journal. You'll be pleasantly surprised how much God uses past works of grace to encourage your childlike faith. Reviewing it is remembering it.

Evaluate the past with childlike faith—When you review your past prayer requests, your childlike faith will grow as you see answers to specific prayers. But it's also important to use these prayer review times to foster childlike trust as you see all of the requests that were not answered as you thought would be best. Remember that God's children don't know what's best for them, but their heavenly Father does. And he doesn't let anything happen to us that's not ultimately best for us.

But as you do all of this, remember that it doesn't take great prayers to make great things happen, it just takes a great God.

DAILY REFLECTION

What kind of journal do you think is best for you?

_____

What kind of prayer writing style works best for you?

_____

_____

How often will you review your prayer journal?

_____

How private do you want your prayers to be?

_____

_____

DAILY PRAYER PROMPT

B—Believe God can do anything.
E—Embrace your childlike identity.
S—Specify your requests.
T—Trust God to do what's best with your requests.

DAILY PRAYER

God, help me write down my prayers. Enable me to review them consistently. Answer a specific prayer request today. Amen.

What specific requests do you need to make for the roles God's given you today?

Role 1: _____

What you'd like to see God do this week:

_____

Role 2: _____

What you'd like to see God do this week:

_____

Role 3: _____

What you'd like to see God do this week:

_____

Role 4: _____

What you'd like to see God do this week:

_____

Role 5: _____

What you'd like to see God do this week:

_____

Role 6: _____

What you'd like to see God do this week:

_____

Top Four Tasks

1. _____

2. _____

3. _____

4. _____

Top Three Thank-Yous

1. _____

2. _____

3. _____

LEARNING TO LOVE OTHERS THROUGH PRAYER

He that loveth little prayeth little, he that loveth much prayeth much.

AUGUSTINE

You also must help us by prayer, so that many will give thanks on our behalf for the blessing granted us through the prayers of many.

2 CORINTHIANS 1:11

We didn't have to teach our kids to care about themselves. From their very first breath, they have been primarily concerned with "me." Long before they could sing Toby Keith's old song "I Wanna Talk About Me," they were living out its message every moment of every day.

That's why, along with every other parent, we have spent countless hours, given countless corrections, and strategized countless ways, trying to teach them to care about others. We want our kids to think about their siblings, their friends, and everyone else's needs and wants—not just their own.

God's the same way with his kids. That's why Jesus builds this others-focused approach into his prayer. Jesus said, "Our Father..." (Matthew 6:9). He could have told us to say, "My Father." But he didn't. Why? Prayer is personal, but it's impact is designed to be public. Jesus wants our prayer to be focused on others as well. Prayer is a community project.

We continue to see this community emphasis throughout the prayer. Every request is in third person. In verse 11, he says, "Give *us* this day *our* daily bread." In verse 12, in regards to forgiveness, he says, "and forgive *us our* debts, as *we* also have forgiven *our* debtors." In verse 13, as he talks about deliverance from temptation and evil, he says, "And lead *us* not into temptation, but deliver *us* from evil." Throughout this prayer, Jesus shows us that it is meant to be a place where we care about others.

God intends for prayer to unite our hearts with his life and the life of those around us. He wants to use prayer to get us thinking about God, our lives, and the lives of others. Our heavenly Father designed prayer to teach us how to love one another.

When we see prayer like this, we understand prayer is meant to grow our capacity to love one another. Because when you start showing enough care for the lives of those around you that you start asking God to help them, you are loving people in a way that is uniquely glorifying to God. Why? It shows that you really believe that he can make a difference in the lives of people and that you genuinely want him to.

Jesus uses prayer to increase our love for each other and the world around us.

Do you pray for others? Do you pray with others?

That's exactly what we see happening in the early days of the church. The book of Acts shows us a praying church. Many people are familiar with all of the amazing events that took place in the book of Acts among those first Christians. But what many of us miss is how prayer dominated the life of that church. Prayer is mentioned more in the book of Acts than in any other book in the Bible. And most of those references are times when the church is praying together for others. God wants us to understand that if we want a powerful, prevailing church, we need a praying church.

With prayer, your impact on the lives of others isn't simply made by natural gifting, it's made by your God. That's why an older saint who can barely move physically but can pray all day can have a greater impact for the kingdom, whether seen or unseen, than the person who can work all day but can't find the time to pray. Everybody can make an eternal impact in the lives of others through prayer.

Unfortunately, many people don't love people with their prayers. Most Christians fail to pray others' problems and plans. Think about how often "you have not because you ask not" is true in the lives of others simply because we haven't asked God to help them?

What if the church started to pray others' dreams and problems? What if we asked others if God had answered the specific prayer we have been praying for them? How cool would it be if we started to regularly celebrate specific answers to prayers in the lives of others?

Think about how much more people would feel loved in that community. Imagine how real God would seem to that community. Can you feel the childlike faith that would mark the hearts of those ordinary people living in the presence of an extraordinary God?

You see, if it's true that "specificity leads to visibility" for us personally, it's also true for our community, group, team, and family.

One of my favorite examples in the book of Acts comes from Acts 12, where Peter was in prison and was about to be executed the next day. What did the church do? They came together and prayed for his deliverance. Think about the childlike faith that it took for those Christians to give up their evening to ask a God they couldn't see to deliver Peter from a Roman unjust judicial system. That's a beautiful picture of "my heavenly Father can do anything" kind of faith.

If you're familiar with the story, you know that God answered the specific prayers of those people and delivered Peter that night! In the middle of the night, the prison doors opened and Peter walked out of that prison. Peter thought he was dreaming. We know that his life was being affected by the loving, specific prayers from others.

We're told that Peter walked into that prayer meeting that night. Can you imagine being one of the ones in that room? How hard do you think it was for some of them to believe it was really Peter? I bet some of them ran to Peter immediately, while others sat stunned. Some jumped with joy, and others cried tears of wonder. Regardless of how they all responded individually, I bet it was an amazing night.

And this isn't just something that is meant to transform your church, increase your church's joy, faith, and more. It can also apply to any group of people. Work teams can start doing this. Sports teams. Families can start doing this. You can start writing down these prayers in your "Roles to Prayer Goals" part of your daily private prayer time with God. As you do this, when appropriate, invite others into your prayer goals. When you do this, God multiplies your joy.

But remember, your specific prayers don't have to be "spiritual." Ask God for what you think is best, and trust him to do what's best with your request.

I'll never forget hearing about what happened in a friend's family in our neighborhood. Nathan, my childhood friend, is a great businessman. He loves to start businesses. But as anyone who does that kind of work knows, sometimes you have to go without a paycheck in the short run to increase the chances that you achieve financial goals in the long run.

Well, unfortunately, Nathan's short run was turning into a long time. It had gotten to the point that he sold his truck to make ends meet and was having his wife give him a ride to work. These kinds of things, obviously, would be hard for anyone to go through, but for a Tennessee redneck who loves his truck just a little less than his family, it was really hard.

Nathan isn't the kind of guy who just sits still and hopes things get better. In fact, Nathan is the kind of guy who struggles to sit still. So he worked harder and harder to improve the financial situation for his family of six. But nothing changed.

So he led his family to make a "Top Ten in November" prayer list. As a family, without anyone outside the family knowing, they would pray for ten specific things to happen that month. I don't remember everything that was on that list, but you better believe "God, give me a truck" was on it.

Think about the childlike faith it took to pray that. Think about the love he felt, knowing that his family was praying that for him.

That month, Nathan got a phone call from one of his neighbors, telling him that they were moving back to California in a few months. Nathan was sad for them to go, since their families had become great friends. But there was a good chance those neighbors would return in a couple of years. So much so, they weren't going to sell their house, just rent it out until they returned.

Before Chris, the neighbor, got off the phone with Nathan, Chris asked him if he'd like to take care of his truck until he returned—his Dodge Ram that could do anything a redneck could think up. Nathan just about dropped the phone. I have to think he felt something like the Israelites did when they were told that God was going to make a way *through* the Red Sea. "What I'm hearing you say is…" "Yeah," Chris said, "it'd be a win-win." Where Chris was going to be living in California, that truck would be more hassle than it was worth. Nathan, of course, said he'd love to take care of his truck!

Nathan told his wife and their kids about the truck that night, mostly while lying on the floor in tears. Can you imagine the joy they felt? The hope? It was a moment where everyone in that room felt the truth, God can do anything. Not, "God used to be able to do anything in biblical times." No. Today. Right now. Where you are. With your problems. With your dreams. He can do anything. And he's often more eager to answer our prayer than we are to ask. Nathan and his family didn't offer up great prayers, they just prayed to a great God.

Chris didn't know about Nathan's prayers. But that's kind of the point, isn't it? Chris didn't need to know about Nathan's over-the-top, "don't see how that can happen" prayers. God did. And as the Bible shows us over and over, God can do more in a moment than we can do in a lifetime.

As awesome as this answer to prayer was for Nathan, it was made even better by the fact that he shared this prayer request with others. He invited them to pray with him and for him. When he was explaining to his family what happened, with tears running down his cheeks, can you imagine how much the childlike faith was growing in their hearts? They felt that their prayers really made a difference in his life. And he felt a deeper love knowing that they actually prayed for him in this specific way.

Prayer is a community project because love is a community need.

I suggest you send a text or email to two people to let them know that you are praying for them. Make it specific and appropriate. Maybe it could be a verse. Maybe something you've learned about them. How awesome would it be if God's children started to do this regularly? How much more loved would people feel? Let's do it!

DAILY REFLECTION

Who can you pray for specifically?

_____

What keeps you from praying for others?

_____

Who are the top five people God put in your life that you can pray
a specific prayer for? Write them a prayer card this week.

_____

What would you like to see God do in your loved ones?

_____

Write a prayer card to others. Tell them that you are thankful for
them and what you are praying specifically happens.

DAILY PRAYER PROMPT

B—Believe God can do anything.
E—Embrace your childlike identity.
S—Specify your requests.
T—Trust God to do what's best with your requests.

DAILY PRAYER

God, help me pray for others. Cause others to see you work in
their lives through my prayers. Enable me to pray for five specific
people today in specific ways. Amen.

What specific requests do you need to make for the roles God's given you today?

Role 1: _____

What you'd like to see God do this week:

_____

Role 2: _____

What you'd like to see God do this week:

_____

Role 3: _____

What you'd like to see God do this week:

_____

Role 4: _____

What you'd like to see God do this week:

_____

Role 5: _____

What you'd like to see God do this week:

_____

Role 6: _____

What you'd like to see God do this week:

_____

Top Four Tasks

1. _____

2. _____

3. _____

4. _____

Top Three Thank-Yous

1. _____

2. _____

3. _____

Today's Two Prayer Texts/Emails

1. _____

2. _____

LEARNING TO PRAY
THROUGHOUT THE DAY

*There is not in the world a kind of life more sweet and
delightful than that of a continual conversation with God.*

BROTHER LAWRENCE

I prayed to the God of heaven. And I said to the king...

NEHEMIAH 2:4-5

When children are young enough to be dependent on their parents for daily bread, but old enough to ask for it, they are at a stage where they have no trouble talking to their parents throughout the day. Parents of kids at this stage know this is true.

The reasons kids normally talk so much at this stage are many. But one of them is that they need help throughout the day.

God's children are the same way. That's why it's important to learn how to pray throughout the day. When you pray "on the go," you increase your awareness of your heavenly Father's presence and power in the midst of your daily moments and, consequently, you also increase your hope, joy, and courage in the face of the ups and downs of life in a broken world.

Prayers on the go can be short or long. They can be specific, or sometimes the specificity is obvious for the vague "help me" prayer. Any decent parent can help their kids in tough situations with vague requests. How much more can our heavenly Father? The point with these types of prayers is to grow your relationship on the go.

Nehemiah, one of the greatest leaders of all time, provides a great picture of how to pray throughout the day. The book of Nehemiah starts with Nehemiah serving as a cupbearer, against his will, for King Artaxerxes. Nehemiah and the people of Israel were an oppressed people. They had no rights. The people at that time would have thought that they didn't have much of a future either.

In chapter 1, Nehemiah heard that the walls of Jerusalem, his hometown, were broken down. These walls had spiritual significance. Nehemiah knew that their destruction ultimately happened because of Israel's rejection of God's ways.

When Nehemiah heard about the broken walls of Jerusalem, he fasted and he prayed. He asked God to help him rebuild the walls. Chapter 1 captures Nehemiah's childlike prayer where he asks God to forgive and help him get permission from the king to rebuild the wall. Think about the childlike faith it took to believe in a God big enough to control the king's heart that was controlling his life!

Not too long after that, when Nehemiah was serving the king, the king asked him if something was wrong. Although Nehemiah was scared, he told the king about how the broken walls had broken his heart. This is what Nehemiah said happened next:

> Then the king said to me, "What are you requesting?" So I prayed to the God of heaven. And I said to the king, "If it pleases the king, and if your servant has found favor in your sight, that you send me to Judah, to the city of my fathers' graves, that I may rebuild it."

The king asked Nehemiah a question. But when kings ask their cupbearers a question, it's important to remember that it's not like you asking a friend a question. Nehemiah felt fear, not freedom, in that moment. So what did Nehemiah do? It says that he "prayed to the God of heaven," and answered the king. It couldn't have been a long prayer. I'm sure it wasn't articulate. But when we keep reading, we know it was answered.

God recorded that for us because he wants us to pray throughout the day. He desires for us to understand that the value of a prayer isn't the length, the wording, or the calmness of the circumstances in which it is offered. The value of a prayer is determined by the God to whom it is offered. Nehemiah's prayer was a short prayer of desperation. It's the kind of prayer we can pray all the time. When we get a text about something that strikes terror in our hearts, an email that frustrates our plans, an encounter with someone that we'd rather not have and don't feel prepared for, or anything like this, God wants us to ask for his help in that moment. He wants us to be like Nehemiah and grow our prayer life on the go.

Do you pray throughout the day?

Many times we don't. Most of us are more prone to worry when we encounter the unexpected everyday problems that everyone faces in a broken world. More times than not, others of us get angry when our expectations don't get met. In these moments, we find it more natural to face our problems as if God hasn't promised to be with us, that he doesn't care to help us, that he'd die in our place but not help us with our day. We act like atheists. We think like cynics.

God wants us to remember that we are his children. And because we are his children, he is with us, for us, and nothing can stop his perfect purposes for us. He wants us to act like a child, just as Nehemiah did.

And Nehemiah's childlike prayer wasn't just seen in that first and second chapter. Later, in chapter 4, when Nehemiah and his team are making significant progress building the wall, they face opposition. Nehemiah 4:8 says, "They all plotted together to come and fight against Jerusalem and to cause confusion in it." This sounds awful!

So what does Nehemiah do? Verse 9 says, "We prayed to our God and set a guard as a protection against them day and night." These guys are working around the clock. But they understood that they needed God's help. Where did they ask for it? On the go.

In the fifth century, the Greek Orthodox Church put together a prayer that they still use to this day. It's called the Prayer of Jesus. It simply states: "Lord Jesus Christ, Son of God, have mercy on me, a sinner." They call these short prayers "breath prayers" because they can be spoken in a single breath. I'm calling them "on the go prayers" or "prayers to go."

If life was so busy back in the fifth century that they needed these breath prayers, don't you think in our busy twenty-first century we need them as well? As we make our way through what C.S. Lewis called the "Kingdom of Noise," let's offer up some "on the go" prayers.

Let me challenge you to pray some "on the go" prayers today. When you do, I'd encourage you to do the following:

Create a category in your daily prayer "roles to goals" for "prayers on the go"—When you write prayers out in the morning and review prayers from the day before, write down any "on the go" prayers from the day before. You won't remember them all, but this will make you more aware than if you don't record them. If you keep an Evernote prayer list, then you can capture some of those throughout the day when you're standing in a long line or bored.

Remind yourself of the childlike prayer principles for each of those moments if you are able—When you pray on the go, remember to believe that God can do anything, you need his help, specificity leads to visibility, and God will do what's best with your request. Reminding yourself of these truths will help you live in a chaotic world without a chaotic heart.

God wants to grow our relationship with him on the go. One of the major ways we show that we have an everyday, all-day relationship with God is by praying throughout the day. God loves to show up for his children in small and large ways throughout their everyday life.

DAILY REFLECTION

What's keeping you from praying throughout the day?

What do you usually do when problems arise? How do you think things would be different if you faced your problems and pursued your plans like Nehemiah?

DAILY PRAYER PROMPT

B—Believe God can do anything.
E—Embrace your childlike identity.
S—Specify your requests.
T—Trust God to do what's best with your requests.

DAILY PRAYER

Father, help me live with an awareness of your helpful presence and my constant need throughout today. Cause me to ask for your help in specific ways. Answer a prayer in a way that would be meaningful to me today. Amen.

What specific requests do you need to make for the roles God's given you today?

Role 1: _____

What you'd like to see God do this week:

_____

Role 2: _____

What you'd like to see God do this week:

_____

Role 3: _____

What you'd like to see God do this week:

_____

*Role 4:*_____

What you'd like to see God do this week:

_____

*Role 5:*_____

What you'd like to see God do this week:

_____

*Role 6:*_____

What you'd like to see God do this week:

_____

Top Four Tasks

1._____

2._____

3._____

4._____

Top Three Thank-Yous

1._____

2._____

3._____

Today's Two Prayer Texts/Emails

1. _____

2. _____

On-the-Go Prayers

_____

_____

_____

_____

_____

_____

THE IMPORTANCE AND POWER
OF PRAYERFUL FASTING

*Fasting helps express, deepens, confirms the resolution
that we are ready to sacrifice anything, even ourselves, to
attain what we seek for the kingdom of God.*

ANDREW MURRAY

"When you fast..."

MATTHEW 6:16

Children can communicate a lot to their parents by their actions. They
can do the dishes, clean up their room, help a sibling with their
homework, take out the trash, allow someone else to get the last piece, or
go first without being asked. These actions are heard loudly by parents.
Parents who find themselves in these rare, hopeful moments are moved
by these actions and want to reward these actions.

Usually, these actions come with a request. The kids want to stay up
later to watch the game, go to a friend's party, or something along these
lines. Parents who find themselves in these rare, hopeful moments usually
want to reward their kids—even if they know their motives aren't completely pure.

A similar dynamic is at play between God and his children when it
comes to fasting. Fasting sounds super spiritual, but it's simply something

that God's children do when they want to communicate with more than words. After studying fasting throughout the Bible, Richard Foster says that "throughout Scripture fasting refers to abstaining from food for spiritual purposes."[7] The great British pastor, Martyn Lloyd-Jones, wrote, "Fasting should really be made to include abstinence from anything which is legitimate in and of itself for the sake of some special spiritual purpose."[8]

Regardless of which definition you find most helpful, I think all of them convey the simplicity of fasting. Each of them communicates the heart of Jesus' message on fasting, which came right after his teaching on prayer. Jesus said,

> When you fast, do not look gloomy like the hypocrites, for they disfigure their faces that their fasting may be seen by others. Truly, I say to you, they have received their reward. But when you fast, anoint your head and wash your face, that your fasting may not be seen by others but by your Father who is in secret. And your Father who sees in secret will reward you (Matthew 6:16-18).

Did Jesus spend any time defining fasting? None. Why? Because it's such a simple concept that it was obvious to every one of the thousands of people who were listening to him beside the Sea of Galilee.

Not only is the concept simple, Jesus wants to make sure that our practice of it is simple too. He says he's not interested in people fasting as a performance for others. He doesn't want us using it to increase our standing in each other's eyes. Instead, Jesus wants our attention to be on "your Father who sees." When God's children fast, they are to focus on their heavenly Father.

And just as with prayer, Jesus points us both to God's presence and to a reward. Jesus doesn't tell us that there are only certain kinds of rewards that our heavenly Father will provide. He just says, "reward." The concept is as big as the heart of God.

One more thing. Notice that Jesus says "when you fast." He didn't say "if you fast." No one heard him saying, "If you're into it, fast some." No. He assumes that you understand that a part of embracing our childlike identity is fasting.

Jesus puts this teaching right after his teaching on prayer. The reason they are so closely connected in his Sermon on the Mount is that they are so closely connected in his mind.

We don't just see this connection between fasting and prayer in the Sermon on the Mount, we see it throughout the Bible. A quick look at the 77 times the Bible talks about fasting shows that Moses prayed and fasted, Israel prayed and fasted, Daniel prayed and fasted, Nehemiah prayed and fasted, Jesus prayed and fasted, the early church prayed and fasted, just to name a few. Fasting is a normal part of a relationship with God in Christ.

Do you fast regularly?

Most Christians I know don't. Not because they are bad people, don't want to follow Jesus, or anything like that. Most of them haven't fasted because they've never slowed down to give it much thought.

When you do slow down enough to think about the biblical teaching on fasting, you'll notice that the Bible doesn't just emphasize the importance of fasting and prayer, it also shows us that God honors in unique ways the requests associated with fasting. When you study fasting, you see that there are often breakthroughs or powerful turning points that take place when someone or a group of people fasts.

Moses fasted for a great length. We are told, "He was there with the LORD forty days and forty nights. He neither ate bread nor drank water. And he wrote on the tablets the words of the covenant, the Ten Commandments" (Exodus 34:28).

Obviously, this fast was a supernatural fast. You can't go without bread and water for 40 days without a miracle. God was doing a unique work. He was giving Moses the law, the Ten Commandments. Kind of a big moment, huh?

While there are parts of Moses's time with God that are unique to Moses in that moment, there are other aspects God intends to carry over into our lives. God doesn't want us to miss the fact that fasting was present at that significant moment, one of the most important moments in all of human history.

But Moses isn't the only example the Bible points us to. Think about Daniel's life. After Daniel had interpreted dreams, been delivered from the lions' den, seen his friends delivered from the fiery furnace, just to name a few amazing chapters in his life, he found himself confused over a vision. What did he do with his confusion? Daniel tells us, "Then I turned my face to the Lord God, seeking him by prayer and pleas for mercy with fasting and sackcloth and ashes" (Daniel 9:3). Daniel is confused so he prays, and he fasts.

After a lengthy prayer, Daniel tells us that God answered his prayers and his fast. Daniel says, "while I was speaking in prayer, the man Gabriel, whom I had seen in the vision at the first, came to me in swift flight at the time of the evening sacrifice. He made me understand, speaking with me and saying, 'O Daniel, I have now come out to give you insight and understanding'" (Daniel 9:21-22).

Again, while there are parts of this that are unique to Daniel, other parts of this story shouldn't be unique to Daniel. God wants all of his children to pray and fast. And he wants us to see that he works uniquely and powerfully in those moments.

These, of course, aren't the only examples of God powerfully blessing a fast. God blessed Israel's fast with a stunning victory over the Edomites (2 Chronicles 20). Before Nehemiah built Jerusalem's broken walls, an achievement that stunned everyone who understood the situation, he fasted (Nehemiah 1:4). Esther's courageous request came after a three-day fast (4:15-17). After Jesus' fast, he overcame the enemy behind all the enemies of God in the wilderness (Luke 4:1-12). The early church fasted before they sent out Paul and Barnabas on their first mission trip, which turned out to be one of the greatest kingdom-advancing seasons in the history of the world (Acts 13:1-3).

Our heavenly Father wants us to fast and wants to bless our fasts.

It's important to remember that fasting should come from a heart that treasures our heavenly Father more than the gifts he can give us. Isaiah, Jeremiah, Zechariah, and Jesus all corrected people who had turned fasting into something it wasn't supposed to be (Isaiah 58:4; Jeremiah 14:11-12; Zechariah 7:4-6; Matthew 6:16).

Does that mean we need to be perfect? No. No one outside of Jesus fasted with a perfectly pure heart. But we do need to be genuine, sincere, childlike.

I've prayed that many people who read this book who have never fasted, much less fasted regularly, would fast at least one time during this 21-day journey. And to help you get started, I've included a few practical thoughts that were helpful to me that came mostly from Ronnie Floyd.

Find your day—Some days we have more flexibility than others. Identify a day on which to carry out your fast. If you're walking through this with a team, group, church, or family, do your best to fast on the same day.

Find your level—When Scripture talks about fasting, it is talking about abstinence from food. That might mean that you miss one meal, or two meals, or all the meals. Perhaps you can't miss any meals? That's okay, you can abstain from something else, such as social media. Whatever it is, find a level that allows you to participate in the fast.

Set specific goals—"Specificity leads to visibility" in our prayer lives and our fasting. Let me encourage you to ask God to answer one to three specific requests. These could be personal prayer goals, team prayer goals, church prayer goals, family prayer goals, or whatever works best for you.

Plan your time—During the time when you would normally do the thing that you are abstaining from, use that time to read Scripture and pray. The examples of fasting in the Bible show us that the people of God "stepped back" in some way so that they could better "step into" God's presence. Let's do the same, whether that is 15 minutes or an hour.

What might God have in store for us if we follow his Word and make fasting a regular part of our relationship with him? How might our lives, our families, our teams, our churches be different? What might God want to do in the lives of other people because we have a "Father who sees" and "rewards" in secret?

Not too long ago, there was a family who wanted their kids to go to a private Christian school. While they were thankful for the public schools their kids had been going to, they thought their kids would benefit greatly from a Christian school. They had prayed for that opportunity to open up for years but couldn't afford it financially.

So one of the parents started fasting, asking God to open a door. Not long after she started regularly fasting for God to make a way, she was told by someone in a random conversation to start the application process. The friend encouraged her that she never knew how God might show up.

So the parents filled out the application and began the process.

Through a series of events, God made the impossible possible. He opened up a pathway for their kids to go to a great school in a way that fit with their budget. They cried tears of joy, the kind of joy that comes from an awareness of God's "I can do anything" presence and power in their lives.

All of their kids loved the new school. They were growing at that new school in ways that the parents prayed they would.

There are many aspects to this story that are unique, just as there were to Moses's fasting story, Daniel's fasting story, and all the rest. But there are aspects that God wants you to share. He wants you to have your own stories of heartfelt prayers and fasting that lead to specific outcomes you could never reach on your own. He wants your fasting to benefit others like the fast that these parents carried out led to great benefits for their kids.

DAILY REFLECTION

How can you plan your fasting time?

_____

What are the biggest challenges to fasting?

_____

If God would do three things for you, your team, your group, your church, what would you want them to be?

_____

What do you want God to do in your life, relationships, and work that you could symbolically say you want more than food?

_____

DAILY PRAYER PROMPT

B—Believe God can do anything.
E—Embrace your childlike identity.
S—Specify your requests.
T—Trust God to do what's best with your requests.

DAILY PRAYER

God, help me know how best to fast. Bless my fast with a specific answer to prayer. Help me make this a regular part of my life. Enable me to see how significant my fast can be in the lives of others. Amen.

What specific requests do you need to make for the roles God's given you today?

Role 1: _____

What you'd like to see God do this week:

_____

_____

Role 2: _____

What you'd like to see God do this week:

_____

_____

Role 3: _____

What you'd like to see God do this week:

_____

_____

*Role 4:*_____

What you'd like to see God do this week:

_____

*Role 5:*_____

What you'd like to see God do this week:

_____

*Role 6:*_____

What you'd like to see God do this week:

_____

Top Four Tasks

1. _____
2. _____
3. _____
4. _____

Top Three Thank-Yous

1. _____
2. _____
3. _____

Today's Two Prayer Texts/Emails

1. _____

2. _____

On-the-Go Prayers

_____

_____

_____

_____

_____

_____

_____

_____

_____

_____

_____

_____

_____

_____

WHEN YOU CAN'T FIND THE WORDS

If I could hear Christ praying for me in the next
room, I would not fear a million enemies. Yet distance
makes no difference. He is praying for me.

ROBERT MURRAY M'CHEYNE

Listen to my words, LORD;
consider my sighing.

PSALM 5:1 (CSB)

Good parents don't wait until their kids ask for help to do good things for them, especially if they are going through a hard time. Whether it is a kid who didn't make the team, had a friend leave them, or some other heartbreaking event that every kid goes through, parents want to help their kids get through those times. They want to make things better. Some parents get a gift, others take the family out for ice cream, but all good parents work to help their kids regardless of whether their kids ask for it.

The same is true of our heavenly Father. He is always "working all things for our good" (Romans 8:28), whether we ask him to in specific ways each day or not. No one can separate us from his love, regardless of whether we prayed that or not (Romans 8:38-39).

These truths are important to keep in mind as we start to pray our problems, plans, Bible passages, and "on the go" prayers daily. Because I've found that there have been times when I have started to believe the lie that "if I don't ask for it, it won't happen." I know that sounds silly, but I've had it happen to me over and over again.

Somehow, somewhere along the way, occasionally my burden-relieving prayer life turns into a burden-producing prayer life. I begin to think I have to give voice to the prayer, whether verbally or in my head, or God won't do above and beyond all I can imagine or think. I've found myself wondering if God might punish me for not praying enough or for not finding the right words at the right time. Without realizing it, every once in a while, my childlike prayer life turns into performance theatre—something Jesus said he's not interested in.

In those moments, I have to remind myself that the Bible teaches that God's work doesn't depend on our words. God doesn't need great prayers to do great things. In those moments when I get off track, I have to remember who I'm praying to matters way more than how well I'm praying—especially in the difficult times.

One of the first places I saw this in Scripture was in Psalm 5. At the very beginning of this psalm, King David says,

> Give ear to my words, O LORD;
>   consider my groaning.
> Give attention to the sound of my cry,
>   my King and my God,
>   for to you do I pray
> (Psalm 5:1-2).

Notice what David asks the Lord to consider. He says consider his "groaning" or "sighing." David goes on to ask God to give attention to the "sound of my cry." What does David want God to consider and give attention to? Not his perfectly formed prayers. No, he wants God to consider his wordless tears, deep breaths, the sounds that he makes in his difficult times.

David is not in a good situation. He isn't happy about his life. Yet, he has a childlike impulse that leads him both to come to God for help and to interpret his wordless ways.

Then, David goes on to say, he'll "watch." He is expectant. He is hopeful. He believes God will do something with his situations even when he doesn't know what to ask for.

Are you weighed down by something today?

You can pray your problem by simply sighing and groaning in God's presence.

Remember, Jesus told his disciples that prayer doesn't exist to inform God, it exists to engage us with the presence of God. As we've seen, Jesus says, "When you pray, do not heap up empty phrases as the Gentiles do, for they think that they will be heard for their many words. Do not be like them, for your Father knows what you need before you ask him" (Matthew 6:7-8).

Jesus lets them know that their heavenly Father is already working on what is best for his children. Prayer isn't about informing an uninformed God, it's about engaging our unengaged hearts. Prayer is about changing our perspective so that we see the world as God does.

Some have used these words by Jesus as a reason not to pray. They think, *If God already knows, what's the point?* But think about it. Jesus, the God-man, is the greatest teacher ever. He knows what he's doing. He didn't tell us this right before he taught us how to pray to destroy our motivation. Jesus wants this to convict and comfort us. He's letting us know that this is a real relationship God's using prayer to invite us into.

And God doesn't just show us this reality here. It's all over the Bible. The Psalms are filled with people crying out to God in prayer. We're not told what exactly people are praying in many difficult situations. For instance, Hannah was childless and desperately wanted a child. Her prayer time was so filled with tears and emotions that a priest accused her of being drunk (1 Samuel 1:12-16). The apostle Paul talked to the Roman Christians about times when "we do not know what to pray for" (Romans 8:26).

When you live life prayerfully in a broken world, you will come across times when you can't find the words. Charles Spurgeon was a pastor who knew great success and great difficulty. He walked with many people through the "valley of the shadow of death" as a man of prayer. But he knew there were times when people couldn't find the words. But after studying God's Word, he wanted people to know that "groanings which cannot be uttered are often prayers which cannot be refused."[9]

So when you can't find the words, remember, God is already working on what's best for you.

The Bible doesn't just point us to a loving Father who is working for our good apart from our words. It also points us to a Savior and a Spirit who are praying for us. The apostle Paul says, "Likewise the Spirit helps us in our weakness. For we do not know what to pray for as we ought, but the Spirit himself intercedes for us with groanings too deep for words" (Romans 8:26).

And not only the Spirit, but the Son of God, Jesus Christ, is praying for us. Romans 8:34 says, "Who is to condemn? Christ Jesus is the one who died—more than that, who was raised—who is at the right hand of God, who indeed is interceding for us." The writer of Hebrews tells us, "Consequently, [Jesus] is able to save to the uttermost those who draw near to God through him, since he always lives to make intercession for them" (Hebrews 7:25).

These verses had a powerful impact on Robert Murray M'Cheyne, a pastor in Dundee, Scotland, who died in 1843 at the age of 29. He served his church for six years before dying of typhus fever.

Andrew Bonar was a friend of M'Cheyne's and a nearby pastor. Within two years of M'Cheyne's death, Andrew had published *Memoir and Remains of Robert Murray M'Cheyne*. That powerful work is still around over 170 years later.

Anyone who knows anything about serious sickness, facing death at a young age, knows that M'Cheyne had some days where he couldn't find the words to pray. But he leaned on passages like the ones above. Reflecting on their truths, he said, "If I could hear Christ praying for me in the next room, I would not fear a million enemies. Yet distance makes no difference. He is praying for me."[10]

M'Cheyne was comforted in his difficulty by the truth that his Savior was praying for him. Ultimately, what was best for M'Cheyne was to be taken into God's satisfying presence earlier than he had planned.

What do you do with your difficult moments, with your seasons of groaning?

When you can't find the words, remember that prayer is meant to be burden relieving, not burden producing. Focus on the Savior and the Spirit who are interceding for you in the Father's presence. Look into the Psalms to find stories and words that God has already put in place to help you press through.

DAILY REFLECTION

What areas of your life make you sigh or groan most often?

_____

Where are you in danger of believing that God works for you only when you ask him?

_____

Where do you need to believe in your heart that God is working beyond your requests?

_____

DAILY PRAYER PROMPT

B—Believe God can do anything.
E—Embrace your childlike identity.
S—Specify your requests.
T—Trust God to do what's best with your requests.

DAILY PRAYER

God, consider my sighing and help me watch expectantly like the psalmist. Enable me to take comfort and courage in the fact that you are working beyond my words, that you are working all things for my good, and that the Spirit and Jesus are interceding for me.

Help me join Jesus and the Spirit in interceding for those in my life right now who can't find the words. Amen.

What specific requests do you need to make for the roles God's given you today?

Role 1: _____

What you'd like to see God do this week:

_____

Role 2: _____

What you'd like to see God do this week:

_____

Role 3: _____

What you'd like to see God do this week:

_____

Role 4: _____

What you'd like to see God do this week:

_____

Role 5: _____

What you'd like to see God do this week:

_____

Role 6: _____

What you'd like to see God do this week:

_____

Top Three Tasks

1. _____

2. _____

3. _____

Top Three Thank-Yous

1. _____

2. _____

3. _____

On-the-Go Prayers

_____

_____

_____

_____

_____

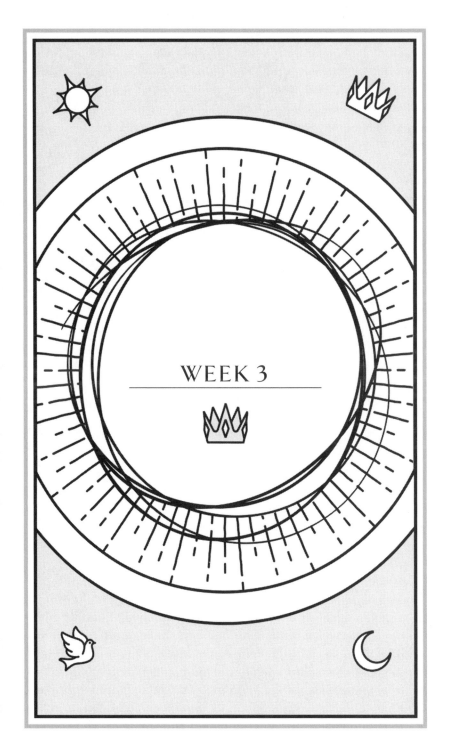

WEEK 3

FIVE SPECIFIC CHILDLIKE
IDENTITY PRAYERS

The Lord's Prayer…serves as an outline of the whole Christian life
by providing certain "fixed points" of concern for the family of God.
It underlines life's priorities and helps us to get them into focus.

SINCLAIR FERGUSON

Be gracious to me, O God, for man tramples on me;
all day long an attacker oppresses me…

PSALM 56:1

Way to go! You've made it through two weeks!

Over the past two weeks, you've started a journey to childlike prayer that can change your world.

Over the first week, you learned that prayer happens best when you believe God can do anything, embrace a childlike identity, specify your requests—praying your Bible, problems, and plans—and trust God to do what's best with your requests.

Last week, you learned habits that foster childlikeness over the long haul. These practices provide the structure needed to build a prayer life that gives you life throughout your life. You saw the importance of a private prayer time with God, writing your prayers, praying for others, praying on the go, remembering how Jesus and the Spirit pray for you, and knowing how to fast.

With these things in place, we are ready to dive a little deeper into the Lord's Prayer. This week, you'll learn the Five Specific Childlike Identity Prayers. Every child of God would greatly benefit from praying these each day. These prayers will focus our hearts each day on what matters most to the roles God has called us to, prepare us for the challenges that await us each day, and propel us further than we ever dreamed possible.

DAILY REFLECTION

What was the best part of last week for you? Why?

_____

What was the hardest part of last week for you? Why?

_____

What prayer goals do you need to make and pray for this coming week?

_____

DAILY PRAYER PROMPT

B—Believe God can do anything.
E—Embrace your childlike identity.
S—Specify your requests.
T—Trust God to do what's best with your requests.

What specific requests do you need to make for the roles God's given you today?

Role 1: _____

What you'd like to see God do this week:

_____

Role 2: _____

What you'd like to see God do this week:

_____

Role 3: _____

What you'd like to see God do this week:

_____

Role 4: _____

What you'd like to see God do this week:

_____

Role 5: _____

What you'd like to see God do this week:

_____

Role 6: _____

What you'd like to see God do this week:

_____

Top Four Tasks

1. _____

2. _____

3. _____

4. _____

Top Three Thank-Yous

1. _____

2. _____

3. _____

Today's Two Prayer Texts/Emails

1. _____

2. _____

On-the-Go Prayers

_____

_____

_____

_____

_____

DAY 16

CHILDLIKE PRAYER #1: PRAYING AS A WORSHIPER

*The worth and excellency of a soul is to be
measured by the object of its love.*

HENRY SCOUGAL

*Hallowed be your name.
Your kingdom come,
your will be done,
on earth as it is in heaven.*

MATTHEW 6:9-10

Jesus uses prayer to teach his people about God's identity and their identity. As we've already seen, God is portrayed as an all-powerful, all-loving Father, and we are his dependent children.

But it's important to notice that Jesus uses the rest of his teaching on prayer to show specific prayers that every child of God should pray. Each of these prayers highlights a characteristic that is included in every child of God's identity.

The first specific prayer request emphasizes the fact that every child of God is a "worshiper." Jesus tells his disciples to pray "hallowed be your name, your kingdom come, your will be done, on earth as it is in heaven" (Matthew 6:9-10). These three requests are all conceptually related. The first request is the most foundational, and the one from which everything else flows. Or, if you know what "nesting dolls" are, the first is the largest one, with each request representing a smaller doll inside.

Unfortunately, many people don't take the time to think about what Jesus is telling us to pray here. They skip over it. It's not a meaningful daily prayer. It's as if they think that the most amazing being in all of human history messed up by starting with this. Surely, we don't really think that.

When we hallow God's name, we treat God as he deserves to be treated. The word for "hallow" is the verb form of "holy." While we don't like the word "holy" in our culture, holiness is where lasting life, joy, peace, and purpose is alone found (Psalm 16:11). To treat God as holy is to treat him as he deserves to be treated, which is what's most important of every moment of every day. His name isn't just letters put together to form a word, it's the essence of who he is. When God's name is being hallowed in our hearts as it should be, then we are all about seeking ways to help his kingdom to come and, as a part of that kingdom, his will to be done.

Tying these three requests together, Jesus teaches us to say, "on earth as it is in heaven." In heaven, God's name is hallowed perfectly. In heaven, God's kingdom is perfect. In heaven, God's kingdom will is done. In heaven, as people relate to God, to each other, to the tasks they have before them, to the management of the possessions that Jesus promised they'd have, as they think about themselves and other things the Bible hasn't told us are happening in heaven right now, God's name is perfectly hallowed and his kingdom will perfectly done.

Jesus teaches us to pray that these heavenly realities come to earth, come to our hearts and lives. Why? Because we need God's help to do God's will, to seek his kingdom purposes, and to hallow his name. We naturally make our way through the day hallowing other people or things in our hearts, seeking to prioritize and pursue other kingdom purposes.

The apostle Paul says that we have "exchanged" what we should hallow, or worship, in our hearts for things we shouldn't. He says, "because they exchanged the truth about God for a lie and worshiped and served the creature rather than the Creator, who is blessed forever! Amen" (Romans 1:25).

Notice that Paul doesn't say we quit or stopped worshiping (worshiping is simply another way of describing "hallowing"). He says that we "exchanged the truth about God for a lie." Our heart is designed by God to hallow the true God, but because of sin, we hallow other things.

I saw the inescapable hallowing function of the human heart most clearly in my kids when they were going through the "night-night" stage. Night-night is what they called a specific blanket that they loved most. It's the blanket that helped them to transform from terrified to tranquil, from unstable to stable, from loud to quiet and content.

We called it the secret weapon. When we dropped the kids off in the children's ministry on Sunday mornings, we told the workers, "If they won't stop crying, bring this blanket out, and they'll be fine in a minute or so." The night-night was undefeated.

And here's the thing about the night-night. There was nothing special about the blanket. We didn't put anything on the blanket, like special oils or fragrances, to get them to like those blankets. All of the kids were given multiple blankets and all of the kids would choose just one of those blankets that would "work."

It wasn't about the blanket, it was about their hearts. Their hearts ascribed a special value to those blankets that wasn't true about those blankets. It was the kiddy version of what Paul was talking about.

As we get older, we leave our blankets behind, but our hearts are still making the same silly exchange—hallowing the creation over the Creator. We base our inner sense of well-being on people's opinions, how much money we have in the bank, how in control we feel, and the like.

Do you know what your night-nights are?

The Bible calls these night-nights idols. And everyone struggles with them. Tim Keller, in his book *Counterfeit Gods*, describes these idols as "anything more important to you than God. Anything that absorbs your heart and imagination more than God."[11]

What might these be? Not usually bad things. They are typically good things.

Some people's hearts and, therefore, days are controlled by the idol of approval. If they are affirmed as they want, then they feel good about life, where it's headed, and the journey they're on. If they're not affirmed, then they feel frustrated, angry, scared, embarrassed, worthless, or some other life-taking emotion.

The Bible affirms the goodness of approval in others' eyes in passages like Proverbs 22:1,

> A good name is to be chosen rather
> than great riches,
> and favor is better than silver or gold.

But sinful hearts have to be careful that this good thing, a "good name," doesn't get turned into a God thing that we have to have, that we base our heart's contentment on. Jesus' name was slandered by almost everyone, but his satisfaction was taken away by no one. If people's opinions and not his heavenly Father's opinion had controlled his purpose, he never would have done what was necessary on the cross to bring salvation to the world.

Do you tend to make an idol out of people's opinions?

Other people don't worry that much about what people think. Instead, their hearts and, therefore, their days are controlled by the idol of productivity. If they are performing as they want to be performing, then they feel good about life, where it's headed, and the journey they're on. If they feel unproductive or behind, they feel frustrated, angry, scared, embarrassed, worthless, or some other life-taking emotion.

God is "pro-productivity." He works, designed humanity to work, created the standards for productivity, and provided tons of instruction in the Bible on how to work. Jesus did the greatest work ever imaginable by purchasing salvation for sinners. But God didn't create any work or work process that he wants you to replace him with. In fact, he commanded us to "rest" from our work so that we'd be reminded that it's his work that makes the kingdom advance.

Do you tend to make an idol out of working?

But there are other people who don't care if they are productive or if people have a high view of them; they struggle instead with the idol of comfort. If they are resting as they want to be resting, then they feel good about life, where it's headed, and the journey they're on. They're more patient and loving toward people when they are in this place. But if they feel uncomfortable or overbooked, they feel frustrated, angry, scared, embarrassed, worthless, or some other life-taking emotion.

God is "pro-comfort." He knows that rest is a good thing, which is why he commanded that we rest one day each week. But he wants us to know that our rest has limits. He wants us to be productive (Colossians 3:23). Do you tend to make an idol out of rest?

Another major way that people take good things and replace God with them is with possessions. People that struggle with the idol of stuff feel good about life, where it's headed, and the journey they're on if they have a certain level of stuff. Their bank account needs to be at a certain amount. Their car, apartment, or house needs to look a certain way. If they aren't at their desired level of stuff, then they feel frustrated, angry, scared, embarrassed, worthless, or some other life-taking emotion.

God loves stuff. After all, he created it! But he doesn't want us to value stuff more than we value him.

Do you tend to make an idol out of stuff?

Everybody struggles at the heart level with some or all of these realities.

When we pray for God's name to be hallowed, his kingdom to come, and his will to be done, we are praying for help in these areas of struggle in our hearts.

Do you ask God to help you overcome your heart idols?

If you are prone to worship and hallow the god of people's opinions, ask God to make your heart hallow his name so much that when others' opinions change, your joy and hope and expectancy don't. Or if everyone is happy with you, that you don't start caring about their opinions more than his.

If you are prone to make an idol out of work, ask God to make your heart hallow his name so much that when you don't feel productive, your joy and hope and expectancy don't disappear, and your sense of well-being isn't gone. Or if you feel super productive or refreshed, that you don't replace him by finding more joy in accomplishment than in him.

If you are prone to make an idol out of comfort, ask God to make your heart hallow his name so much that when you feel overbooked or maxed out, your joy and hope and expectancy don't disappear, and your sense of well-being isn't gone. Or if you feel super refreshed, that you don't replace him by finding more joy in your circumstantial comfort than in him.

If you are prone to make an idol out of possessions, ask God to make your heart hallow his name so much that when you have less than you want, your joy and hope and expectancy don't disappear. Or if you have more than you want, your heart doesn't replace God with the stuff he is providing you.

When you pray for God's name to be hallowed, you are praying that your heart would be free. You're praying that you would be like Jonathan Edwards was when he was fired and it was said of him, "his happiness was out of reach from his enemies."[12] In that moment, his heart hallowed the right God.

When you pray this way, three things typically happen. First, you become more humble in victory because you know that the victory belongs to the awesome Lord you are hallowing and that he is greater than any victorious moment. Second, you become more hopeful in loss because you know that the Lord won't leave you in a loss and that his presence is greater than any victorious moment or reward. Third, you become purposeful in everything because you know, whether you won or lost, God has created you and given you the coming moments to glorify him, and anything you do for his glory is not in vain (1 Corinthians 15:58).

And as you pray this, remember that you aren't praying this just for yourself, you are praying this for others. Jesus started from the very beginning of his prayer by emphasizing the need for us to think of others. He said "Our Father," not "My Father." That community emphasis continues throughout the prayer.

That means friends, fellow church members, coworkers, and family members should pray this prayer for one another. All of us fail to do this perfectly. When someone's failure to do this perfectly impacts you negatively, don't get frustrated with their imperfections. God isn't allowing their imperfections to affect you so that you'd attack them or look down on them, but so that you would pray for them. George Whitefield used to pray for his enemies, "Enlarge their hearts."[13] Help their hearts, God, hallow your name. That's the core problem—the failure to hallow God's name—of every problem in our world.

When you look at these first few requests in light of all this, you can see that these prayers are incredibly practical.

When you find yourself in a situation where your day isn't going as you planned, your main battle will be over whether your heart will hallow God and his kingdom plans—most of which you can't see or understand—or your plans and your will. Our natural impulse is to think *I know what's best for me, and this isn't it.* And if you stay in that thought, it'll ruin the rest of the day.

But by God's grace, as you pray this prayer, you can hallow God and his plans more than your own. You can step in line with the rest of heaven, which is already doing that, and follow a satisfying God through the ups and downs of this particular day. Because of this, you can face the challenges of the day joyfully, lovingly, and productively.

Practically, when you find yourself in this kind of situation, take the three steps we need to take to hallow God's name in our hearts each day. *First*, identify your idols. Question yourself when you are frustrated and anxious. Get to the root of it. Are you hallowing your plans more than your God? To what or to whom are you giving the power to take your contentment away from you?

Second, disarm your idols. Embrace the truth that you don't need your plans to work in order for your heart to find the joy and satisfaction and security that it's looking for—that alone can be found in God.

Third, replace your idols. Recommit your life and your day to God and his purposes. When you do this, you enable your heart to find the source of life, hope, courage, and focus that it needs. This exercise will keep you from denying with your life what you declare with your lips—that God is all you need to be content.

But how can a holy God help unholy people hallow his name without becoming unholy himself? That's one of the greatest challenges that's ever existed from heaven's perspective. The reason a holy God can help unholy people hallow his name without becoming unholy himself is found in Christ. Let's not forget or take for granted the fact that on the cross Jesus took the punishment, the horrors of hell, that we deserved so that he could give us the blessings, the happiness of heaven, that he deserves in eternity. Jesus, the son of God, was treated like an enemy of God on the cross so that the enemies of God, you and me, could be treated like children of God in heaven. Jesus was slandered on earth so that he could give us a good name in heaven. When we see what Jesus did, is doing, and will do in more and more of its awesome glory, we'll start praying this prayer with greater frequency and sincerity. And as those prayers happen, God's name will be hallowed more and more. And as that happens, our homes, relationships, churches, work places, groups, teams, and world will become a happier place.

I love the way Augustine describes the moment he first hallowed God's name in his heart. He said,

> How sweet all at once it was for me to be rid of *those fruitless joys* which I had once feared to lose…! *You drove them from me*, you who are the true, the *sovereign joy.* You drove them from me and took their place, you who are *sweeter than all pleasure*, though not to flesh and blood, you who outshine all light, yet are hidden deeper than any secret in our hearts, you who surpass all honor, though not in the eyes of men who see all honor in themselves…O Lord my God, my Light, my Wealth, and my Salvation.[14]

When we pray for God's name to be hallowed, we are praying for people to have the kind of experience Augustine had. Augustine's encounter with Jesus changed his life. And he wanted to help others experience Jesus in this way. He wanted them to know that receiving Jesus' gift of salvation by faith doesn't change just your eternal destiny; it changes your heart's daily reality. He said, "You have made us for yourself, and our hearts are restless till they find their rest in Thee."[15]

Have you committed your life to Jesus? Have you asked Jesus to save you? He always answers that prayer with a yes!

But after you become a Christian, you still pray for God's name to be hallowed in your heart. You see, when we put our faith in Jesus, the penalty for our sin is removed, the power of sin is broken, but the presence of sin remains. And one of the daily ways that we sin is by not giving God his rightful place in our hearts. Because of this, our relationships with others, our work, our stuff, and so many other things are messed up and made more difficult.

If you don't figure out what really controls your heart, you won't be able to figure out what controls your day. And if you can't figure out what controls your day, you won't figure out what controls your life. And if you can't figure out what controls lives, you don't know what is controlling your church, family, and business. That's why Jesus starts his prayer by teaching us to ask for help to hallow God's name.

DAILY REFLECTION

Which idols do you struggle most with?

_____

What do you sacrifice in service to your idol? Health? Money? Generosity?

_____

What do you do when an idol is threatened?

_____

How can you do something better?

_____

What is a specific prayer that you can pray for you that will better help you hallow God's name in your daily life?

_____

DAILY PRAYER PROMPT

B—Believe God can do anything.
E—Embrace your childlike identity.
S—Specify your requests.
T—Trust God to do what's best with your requests.

DAILY PRAYER

God help me hallow your name in my heart. Enable me to identify and remove your unqualified competition from my heart today. Cause me to live freely for you. Help me lead others to hallow your name as they should as well. Amen.

What specific requests do you need to make for the roles God's given you today?

Role 1: _____

What you'd like to see God do this week:

_____

Role 2: _____

What you'd like to see God do this week:

_____

Role 3: _____

What you'd like to see God do this week:

_____

Role 4: _____

What you'd like to see God do this week:

_____

Role 5: _____

What you'd like to see God do this week:

_____

Role 6: _____

What you'd like to see God do this week:

_____

Top Four Tasks

1. _____

2. _____

3. _____

4. _____

Top Three Thank-Yous

1. _____

2. _____

3. _____

Today's Two Prayer Texts/Emails

1. _____

2. _____

On-the-Go Prayers

_____

_____

_____

_____

_____

_____

_____

_____

_____

_____

_____

_____

_____

_____

_____

_____

_____

_____

_____

CHILDLIKE PRAYER #2:
PRAYING AS A SERVANT

God's work done in God's way will never lack God's supply.

HUDSON TAYLOR

Your kingdom come,
your will be done,
on earth as it is in heaven.

MATTHEW 6:10

J esus uses his teaching on prayer to remind God's children that they
are worshipers in need of God's help to worship rightly. But he also
teaches God's children that they are servants in need of God's help to
serve faithfully.

When Jesus teaches us to pray for God's kingdom to come and his will
to be done, he's teaching us to pray about every area of our life. Some of
those areas will be emphasized in the second part of the prayer. Other areas
are emphasized throughout the rest of Scripture.

One of the key areas emphasized throughout the rest of Scripture concerning kingdom life has to do with our work. Servants work. From the
very beginning of the Bible, God shows us that he designed humanity to
work and that our work is designed to advance his kingdom purposes.

In Genesis 1 and 2, God creates the universe, the Garden of Eden on
earth, and humanity in the Garden of Eden. In his book *According to Plan*,

Australian theologian Graeme Goldsworthy rightly observes that the Garden of Eden is the first picture of the kingdom, which can be defined as "God's people in God's place under God's rule."[16]

Immediately, God commands Adam and Eve, who are made in God's image, to get to work for six out of seven days, just as he does. We're told, "God blessed them. And God said to them, 'Be fruitful and multiply and fill the earth and subdue it, and have dominion over the fish of the sea and over the birds of the heavens and over every living thing that moves on the earth'" (Genesis 1:28).

This statement, which is called the "cultural mandate," is Adam and Eve's kingdom-advancing mission. They are to grow their family, and subdue and exercise dominion over the earth. This necessarily will involve the mundane everyday activities that we all have to do to make family life work. It would include working the ground. It would include every area of life. That's the first picture God shows us of his kingdom purposes. Adam and Eve were created to live with a perfect work-rest balance as they advanced God's kingdom will throughout the earth.

But, sadly, they fail to advance God's kingdom purposes as they should. Instead of doing the work they were supposed to do, which included exercising dominion over "every living thing that moves on the earth," they are dominated by the serpent in Genesis 3. A lot of things are happening in that chapter, but it's important for our purposes to note that they failed to do the work God had given them to do. Because of their failure, God says their kingdom-advancing work will be more difficult. The creation won't comply with their efforts.

In these two early snapshots of the start of the world, God shows us that work has dignity as a kingdom-advancing activity and that it is difficult because of sin and the enemy's kingdom purposes. The work-rest balance is no longer perfect. Sin sabotages our work and our rest. Work now becomes a place of pain and frustration. Envy and anger are present now, although they were never intended to be.

Adam and Eve's sons, Cain and Abel, show us how problematic work became. God tells us that Cain worked the ground and Abel was a shepherd. But Cain gets jealous of Abel's work and the way it was received before God, the benefits that Abel got, so he killed him (Genesis 4:1-16).

This horrifying scene has much to say, but for our purposes, it's important to notice how far work has fallen from its original design.

As we look across our broken world, all of us can easily see that work can be both great and horrible. Leland Ryken, in his helpful book titled *Redeeming the Time: A Christian Approach to Work and Leisure*, finds that people either tend to make too much of work and too little of rest or too little of work and too much of rest. Some people "overwork" while others "underwork." The first group treats work as if it's a god and the second group treats work as if it's gross. Workaholics try to get too much out of work and those who don't take work seriously enough tend to get too little out of work. When someone treats work like a god, they can't take days off consistently. When someone treats work like it's gross, they can't work hard consistently.

Both of those approaches were present throughout the Old Testament. Some people needed to be told to work more as God intends. Solomon, one of the wisest people to ever live, was doing just that when he wrote:

> Go to the ant, O sluggard;
>   consider her ways, and be wise.
> Without having any chief,
>   officer, or ruler,
> she prepares her bread in summer
>   and gathers her food in harvest.
> How long will you lie there, O sluggard?
>   When will you arise from your sleep?
> (Proverbs 6:6-8).

Others needed to be told to work less and rest more. Solomon was emphasizing this truth when he said:

> Unless the LORD builds the house,
>   those who build it labor in vain.
> Unless the LORD watches over the city,
>   the watchman stays awake in vain.
> It is in vain that you rise up early
>   and go late to rest,
> eating the bread of anxious toil;

for he gives to his beloved sleep
(Psalm 127:1-2).

Everybody tends to make one of these two mistakes. Which do you make? Do you work too much and rest too little, or the opposite?

Jesus knows that we will struggle here. That's why it's so important that we pray for our work and for our rest. When Jesus teaches us to pray for God's kingdom to come and his will to be done, he is teaching us to pray that our work advances God's kingdom will as it was originally designed to do. Not just our "spiritual work," but all of our work because God's kingdom will encompasses all of our lives. Even the following requests for "daily bread," "relational grace," and "deliverance from evil" have work as a backdrop.

Making bread in the first century took hours of work once you had all the ingredients. It took even more work outside in the fields before you could begin the breadmaking. When someone prays for daily bread in an agrarian culture with no grocery stores, they are praying for help with their work. The relational difficulties that we are asking grace for happened often in that work process. After all, that's what happened with Cain and Abel. Abel was killed in the working fields. The evil we need deliverance from is evil that impacts our work. Remember, the failure in the Garden of Eden was a failure to do the work God had given Adam and Eve to do. Jesus uses his daily prayer to teach us to pray for our work daily.

When we start asking God to help us advance his kingdom will as we serve with our work and with our rest, several things happen.

First, this prayer causes us to work with greater passion. Nobody gets excited about working on a project they know won't matter. But if you believe that what you do really matters, can really make a difference, is really a part of something great, you get energized. All of God's children have a meaningful role to play in advancing God's kingdom. The apostle Paul writes, "Therefore, my beloved brothers, be steadfast, immovable, always abounding in the work of the Lord, knowing that in the Lord your labor is not in vain" (1 Corinthians 15:58).

This command reflects the fact that all the children of God share a "double calling" from God. We share what theologians have described as a "general calling" from God, things that should be true of every child of

God. This involves a call to love, tell the truth, work for justice, use our words wisely, and more in every situation we are in. But the children of God also have a "particular calling" from God, which is the unique way a person works out their general calling. We aren't all called to be pastors, parents, football players, teachers, accountants, but some of us are. That's our particular calling.

Are you doing dishes for God's kingdom? If you are, the Bible says that your labor is not in vain. That is, your work has meaning. It counts. It matters. In Christ, doing the dishes for God's kingdom is more significant than running a country, winning a Super Bowl, or anything else our world measures as greatness outside of Christ's kingdom purposes. That's hard for us to believe, but it is the claim of Scripture.

This is an important truth, especially for those of us that see work as gross. If we overvalue work and undervalue rest, we need to remember to ask God to enable us to be someone who is "always abounding in the work of the Lord," in the unique way that he has created us.

Second, this prayer causes us to work with greater integrity. When we genuinely pray for God's kingdom will to come through our work, we show our awareness that our holy God is with us at work. He sees and evaluates everything we do. He loves us too much to let us get away with doing the wrong things with our work. He lets us know that how we work really matters.

The apostle Paul told the Corinthian Christians, "each one's work will become manifest, for the Day will disclose it, because it will be revealed by fire, and the fire will test what sort of work each one has done. If the work that anyone has built on the foundation survives, he will receive a reward. If anyone's work is burned up, he will suffer loss, though he himself will be saved, but only as through fire" (1 Corinthians 3:13-15). If you want to do work that's a part of something great, you have to understand that the standards are great. Jesus wants us to work with seriousness and integrity.

Third, when we pray for God's kingdom will to advance through our work, we work with greater freedom. Many people don't work with a heart-level freedom because they tie their identity to their work outcomes. If they succeed, they believe they are a success. If they fail, they believe they are a failure. They have to win or they don't know who they are. They don't usually use that language, but you see it in their lack of inner stability in the face of uncertainty and disappointment.

But this prayer starts by reminding us of the awesome, blood-bought identity that we have in Christ—not because of our achievements, but because of Christ's achievements that we receive by faith (Ephesians 2:8-10). We don't work *for* an identity that we can feel good about, we work *from* an identity that we can feel good about.

This blood-bought identity, a child of God, means that we don't have to "win" to feel good about ourselves, even though we strive to do our best in all things (1 Corinthians 10:31; Colossians 3:23). It also means that we don't have to fear "losing," because the best future for us doesn't depend on our performance, it depends on our Father's will. If we end up in that worst case scenario that we all tend to have in the back of our minds, we can be assured that God will be with us, working all things for our good (Romans 8:28,31-39; Psalm 23).

When these truths sink into our hardworking hearts, we learn to do a better job of resting. True rest comes from trusting God, not buying into the delusional idea that we can control our lives. When we really believe God can do more in a moment than we can do in a lifetime, that he always does what's best for his kids, we can trust him enough to work hard and rest deeply.

Finally, when we pray for God's kingdom will to advance through our work, we work with greater humility. If we are asking for God's help to do our work, we are attacking the pride in our hearts that says we can do what we need to do without God's help. When we walk in awareness of that fact, it makes us hardworking and humble. We are hardworking because we are following God's call on our lives to advance his kingdom will through our work. We are humble because we know that it's God's grace enabling us to do any lasting good in this broken world.

It causes us to be like the apostle Paul who said, "By the grace of God I am what I am, and his grace toward me was not in vain. On the contrary, I worked harder than any of them, though it was not I, but the grace of God that is with me" (1 Corinthians 15:10). Did you catch that? Paul "worked harder than any of them" and, at the same time, he could say "it was not I, but the grace of God that is with me." Hardworking. Humble.

Both characteristics are needed in our broken world. And when we pray for God's help with our work, we position ourselves to be both.

Of course, the question usually sits on the back row of most of our minds, how can we really trust God? After all, our work hasn't earned that trust, has it? Actually, when we think about what our work has earned, it's quite frightening. We're told that "the wages of sin is death" (Romans 6:23a). Sin is our work apart from God's miraculous life-changing grace.

That's why it's so important to remember Christ's work and earnings that get credited to our accounts when we place our faith in him. Jesus is the only one who worked perfectly every moment of every day. Adam and Eve failed, Israel failed, we've all failed, but Jesus succeeded. Jesus said, "Truly, truly, I say to you, the Son can do nothing of his own accord, but only what he sees the Father doing. For whatever the Father does, that the Son does likewise" (John 5:19). Only Jesus was obedient to the Father's will at every moment of every day. Paul tells us that he was "obedient to the point of death, even death on a cross" (Philippians 2:8).

So why did he die on a cross? Jesus died on the cross for our sins. Because we aren't enough to merit God's eternal favor, God sent his Son to earn that favor for us. He was obedient to God's kingdom will where we failed to be. And he was punished for our failures where we deserved to be. But he was raised from the grave, showing us that God wasn't against him, he was against our sin. He was for us and now he could save us. Jesus looked like a failure on the cross so that he could make failures like you and me look like successes in heaven.

Have you received Christ's perfect work by faith? Simply surrender your work record, your control of your life, and ask him to save you. Collapse into his gracious arms by faith. Receive the gift of his Holy Spirit to change you from the inside out.

And continue to look to Jesus' great work, not only to save you from your sins but to help you overcome your sins today. Ask him to help you work today in a way that advances his kingdom work in the places that he's placed you. Plead with him to help you avoid the lie that says what you do, no matter what area of life it is, doesn't matter to him and his kingdom purposes. Fight the lie that says your heavenly Father doesn't want to help you with your daily work.

And remember, it doesn't take great prayers to see God do great things in any area of life, including your work. Simple prayers to a spectacularly awesome God enable you to make a significant impact, no matter where you come from.

One of my favorite stories that illustrates this truth comes from the life of George Washington Carver. In the early 1860s, George Washington Carver was born into slavery. His parents, Mary and Giles, were purchased for $700 in 1855 by Moses Carver. While a baby, George, his sister, and his mother were kidnapped by night raiders from Arkansas. His owner tracked George down, but the others could not be found.

After slavery was abolished in 1865, George struggled to get access to the opportunities many white people had. He still wasn't allowed to go to white schools, so he had to travel farther to black schools. Eventually he was ready to head to college. Unfortunately, simply because he was black, he would get turned away.

Yet, in spite of all the evils of racism that he had to endure, George grew and learned about everything he could. He focused more on what he believed God was calling him to, what God would help him do, than on what others did to him.

And he had an incredible scientific mind. His work with flowers and plants led him to be the first black student at Iowa State. Later, he became the first black faculty member at Iowa State. Carver went on to be celebrated far and wide for his work with plants. He was inventive and creative.

While there certainly was a lot that went into Carver's amazing story, one of the things he was known for was his prayer for insightful ideas for his work. It's said that he would start the day by asking God to reveal secrets to him about plants and vegetables. He prayed, "Mr. Creator, show me the secrets of your universe."

He says that God replied to him by saying, "Little man, you're not big enough to know the secrets of my universe, but I'll show you the secret of the peanut."[17]

Carver went on to discover 300 new uses for peanuts. He prayed for help as he worked with sweet potatoes as well. God blessed his work and helped him discover 115 products from it.

He enjoyed many other amazing opportunities because of his fantastic work. He didn't pray great work prayers, just his simple "show me your secrets" prayer to a great God, and great things happened.

Maybe you have a long list of achievements without a long history of praying your work plans. Don't compare yourself with others, compare yourself with what you would be if you prayed more for your work. Is that easy? No. But that's reality. How much of "you have not because you ask not" is true of your work? We'll know in eternity. But until then, let's ask God to help us work as he originally designed our lives to work.

DAILY REFLECTION

What secrets and insights and ideas do you want God to reveal to you today as he did for George Washington Carver?

_____

How can God start helping you at work?

_____

What do you think might happen if you start praying a simple prayer each day for your work?

_____

Do you believe God can give you ideas that will help you accomplish your work goals that you won't have without his help?

_____

Do you believe you need his help with your work?

_____

_____

_____

DAILY PRAYER PROMPT

B—Believe God can do anything.
E—Embrace your childlike identity.
S—Specify your requests.
T—Trust God to do what's best with your requests.

DAILY PRAYER

God, help me with my work. Cause me to see work as a calling from you to represent you. Bring to mind ways that I can approach my work more like you want me to. Help me to remember Jesus doing the most important work. Amen.

What specific requests do you need to make for the roles God's given you today?

Role 1: _____

What you'd like to see God do this week:

_____

Role 2: _____

What you'd like to see God do this week:

_____

*Role 3:*_____

What you'd like to see God do this week:

_____

*Role 4:*_____

What you'd like to see God do this week:

_____

*Role 5:*_____

What you'd like to see God do this week:

_____

*Role 6:*_____

What you'd like to see God do this week:

_____

Top Four Tasks

1._____

2._____

3._____

4._____

Top Three Thank-Yous

1. _____

2. _____

3. _____

Today's Two Prayer Texts/Emails

1. _____

2. _____

On-the-Go Prayers

_____

_____

_____

_____

_____

_____

_____

_____

_____

CHILDLIKE PRAYER #3:
PRAYING AS A MANAGER

*He is no fool who gives what he cannot
keep, to gain what he cannot lose.*

JIM ELLIOT

Give us this day our daily bread.

MATTHEW 6:11

Jesus teaches God's children that they are worshipers in need of God's help to worship rightly, servants in need of God's help to serve faithfully, and managers in need of God's help to steward God's stuff.

Right after Jesus tells his disciples to pray for God's name to be hallowed, his kingdom to come, and his will to be done, on earth as it is in heaven, he says to ask for "daily bread."

When you first read this prayer, this seems like a major shift, doesn't it? It seems like the request for daily bread is the kind of request that you don't bring up in the room where everybody is talking about kingdom-advancing purposes.

But not in Jesus' kingdom. Jesus continues to emphasize the Father-child nature of the conversation that frames his approach to prayer. He wants us to understand that heaven cares about what's happening in your home. Heaven cares about your hunger. He wants us to think of our heavenly Father when we think about food.

This shouldn't come as too big of a surprise to those familiar with the Bible. After all, where was the kingdom lost in Genesis 3? What was the battle over what Adam and Eve lost? Food. Provision. Adam and Eve rejected God's will and God's provision and took a bite of forbidden food. They listened to their appetites more than the Creator of those appetites, and the consequences were disastrous.

Adam and Eve forgot who they were. They wanted to "be like God" (Genesis 3:5). They wanted to be in charge. They didn't want to be dependent kids.

Jesus is using this prayer for provision to remind us each day of who we are. We are God's children. And we are children who need our heavenly Father to provide bread for us. We are dependent. And if we need our heavenly Father to provide something as simple as daily bread, you better believe we need him to provide everything else.

When you understand you are at this stage of childhood, it changes your perspective on your possessions. You recognize that you are at the stage that one of my friend's kids was at when my friend was explaining to the child, who didn't want his dad to have something that was "his," that "everything you have, I own."

Jesus' half-brother James made this point too when he said, "Do not be deceived, my beloved brothers. Every good gift and every perfect gift is from above, coming down from the Father of lights, with whom there is no variation or shadow due to change" (James 1:16-17).

Do you see everything you own as a gift from God to steward for his name and his kingdom?

If you do, then you can avoid making one of the two major errors people have made historically with their stuff—asceticism or materialism. Asceticism sees stuff as almost always bad. Materialism sees stuff as almost always good. Randy Alcorn, author of *Money, Possessions, and Eternity*, says that "both result in excesses that undermine rather than further kingdom purposes."[18]

The person who sees money and wealth as always bad fails to recognize the goodness of God's gifts and the good that can be brought about by rightly using God's gifts. The person who sees money and wealth as almost always good fails to recognize the significant ongoing impact of sin that twists God's good gifts for less than God glorifying purposes.

Alcorn points his readers to the Bible's teaching on all of this and concludes that it calls for us to have a stewardship mentality. A steward's or a manager's "primary goal is to be found faithful by his master as the steward uses the master's resources to accomplish the tasks delegated to him."[19] Or, to put it another way, your relationship with God should change your relationship with your stuff. God's children manage their heavenly Father's stuff.

When you start to embrace this new prayer perspective on possessions, it changes you in three major ways. *First*, this prayer makes you more grateful. When you genuinely believe that all you have you have received from God, none of which you deserve, you become grateful. Our world tends to be marked by grumbling and complaining, not gratitude. Like Adam and Eve, we tend to ignore the many great things God has given us and focus on the one tree or thing or person he hasn't yet given us. Jesus uses this prayer to foster daily gratitude.

Second, this prayer makes you bolder with your prayers. When you truly understand that you have a Father in heaven who loves you, who created all things out of nothing, who controls all things, who has given you every heart beat that you have, and always does what's best for you, you become bolder with your requests.

When kids are at the stage where they need their parents to provide daily bread and everything else, they don't think about the budget. They just ask. They're bold.

The writer of Hebrews encouraged this childlike boldness, writing, "Let us then with confidence [boldness] draw near to the throne of grace, that we may receive mercy and find grace to help in time of need" (Hebrews 4:16).

What kind of father wants to hear requests only about "spiritual" matters? We wouldn't admire that father. And yet so often we do that with our heavenly Father. Ask him for whatever you want. If it's not best for you, you won't get it. But my guess is that you have plenty of things in your life right now that he's already given you that don't qualify as "spiritual" on your scorecard. Your heavenly Father cares about all of your life. Pray in a way that shows you believe that by being bold.

Third, this prayer makes you more generous with your possessions. How? If you trust God will provide for you in a way that is best tomorrow, you will be more generous today. If you don't trust him to provide you with the life that is best for you, you won't be generous today. It's that simple. Greedy people don't trust God to provide the life that is best for them. Generous people do.

The stats that say we are both the wealthiest people in the history of the world and, at the same time, the least generous in a long time are, at the heart, a trust problem. This daily prayer for daily bread is designed to help foster childlike trust that leads to generosity.

I'll never forget one vacation Bible school at our church when my wife, Melanie, found a $20 bill in the parking lot. An offering was being taken that night to help some people in need. And the kids were challenged to give something to it.

Melanie checked around with different volunteers working that night and found out whose it was. It turns out that the kid who brought the money brought all the money that he had to his name.

Why in the world would someone do that? Everything? Here's how. Because he trusted his parents to continue to provide for him tomorrow, he was generous today.

Jesus doesn't tell us that we have to give everything away like that kid, but he does want us to have the same trust in our hearts toward our heavenly Father. How do you know when you have that trust? When you become more generous today because your Father has been generous to you.

Of course, we all fail in this area, don't we? The answer isn't to try harder. Although more effort is important, it's not enough. No. We need to look to the Father's generosity. When we see that Jesus, although rich, became poor so that he could make us, the poor, rich eternally, it will begin to change our hearts. We'll simultaneously become more grateful, more courageous, and more generous. If he did that for us all those years ago, we'll see how silly it is to think that he'd leave us today, tomorrow, or 10,000 years from now. It will help us avoid living like a modern-day

Scrooge in a world filled with Tiny Tims. It will help us avoid missing the moments *today* that God wants us to steward as we steward his stuff for his glory.

As you ask God to provide, remember, it doesn't always have to make sense to the world around you. One of my favorite examples of this type of prayer life comes from the life of George Müller.

Although George Müller was a pastor for over 60 years, he was known most widely for the way he cared for orphans. He started an orphanage that helped thousands and thousands of orphans during the mid-nineteenth century in England. After his death, one newspaper said about him and his orphan care, he "robbed the cruel streets of thousands of victims, the jails of thousands of felons, and the poorhouses of thousands of helpless waifs."[20] His life counted for the cause of Christ.

But the thing that made Müller's incredible work so unique was the way that he provided for all of those orphans and the various ministries that he led. The first guideline that he followed for fundraising was simply to ask God to provide: "No funds should ever be solicited. No facts or figures concerning needs are to be revealed by the workers in the orphanage to anyone except to God in prayer."[21] If that didn't sound strange enough, he also didn't take a salary the last 68 years of his ministry, trusting God to provide through people as he prayed for it.

As strange as all this sounds, that's what he did. It is estimated that God provided what would be the equivalent of millions of dollars today for Müller through his prayers. Many of Müller's prayers can be read in his autobiography. Müller believed God could do anything, embraced his childlike identity, specified his prayers, and trusted God to do what was best with his requests.

While I don't believe the Bible calls us all to take the exact same approach to life and ministry that Müller did, I believe with all my heart that it calls us to have the same childlike view of God as a trustworthy provider every day of our lives.

Just a few weeks before I wrote this chapter, someone who is a member of the church I lead felt led to start praying that God would provide a new car for a coworker who was going through a really tough time.

She had a car, but it wasn't reliable enough to get all the way to where her dad was, who was struggling with a serious sickness. It often shut off at stoplights. To make matters worse, her husband had been jobless for quite a while because his industry was basically shut down during the COVID-19 crisis. She had two teenage daughters, one of whom had significant special needs.

The family who was a part of our church started praying a version of the prayer we are talking about in this chapter. And as they asked God to provide for the coworker, God began to move their hearts to try to help get her a reliable car.

By God's grace, God answered their prayers by helping them raise money for a reliable car, making a car dealer give them a great deal, and providing funds that covered the taxes and insurance for the car for two years!

When the woman received the gift, she cried tears of joy. She told the folks providing the car how this was an answer to their prayers, that God is a faithful provider, and that one day she hoped to be able to bless others in this way.

My friend was blown away with the over-the-top way God answered their prayers and allowed them to be a part of the answer to those prayers. Our Father is in the heavens and he can do anything. Let's make sure our prayers for provision show that we believe that.

DAILY REFLECTION

Do you struggle more with ascetism or materialism? Where do you see that?

_____

How might a stewardship perspective change areas that need to change in your relationship with your stuff?

_____

If you believed that God would provide you with five things that you think would really bless you, what would those be?

_____

_____

DAILY PRAYER PROMPT

B—Believe God can do anything.
E—Embrace your childlike identity.
S—Specify your requests.
T—Trust God to do what's best with your requests.

DAILY PRAYER

God, help me see you as my provider. Enable me to ask you for good gifts. Protect me from misusing the stuff you have entrusted to me by either making too much or too little of it. Help me see stuff as something that can advance your purposes in my life and the lives around me. Amen.

What specific requests do you need to make for the roles God's given you today?

Role 1: _____

What you'd like to see God do this week:

_____

Role 2: _____

What you'd like to see God do this week:

_____

Role 3: _____

What you'd like to see God do this week:

_____

Role 4: _____

What you'd like to see God do this week:

_____

Role 5: _____

What you'd like to see God do this week:

_____

Role 6: _____

What you'd like to see God do this week:

_____

Top Four Tasks

1. _____

2. _____

3. _____

4. _____

Top Three Thank-Yous

1. _____

2. _____

3. _____

Today's Two Prayer Texts/Emails

1. _____

2. _____

On-the-Go Prayers

_____

_____

_____

_____

_____

_____

_____

_____

_____

CHILDLIKE PRAYER #4:
PRAYING AS A PEACEMAKER

To be a peacemaker, you must know the peace giver.

BILLY GRAHAM

Forgive us our debts,
as we also have forgiven our debtors.

MATTHEW 6:12

P rayer shows us that God's children are worshipers in need of God's help to worship rightly, servants in need of God's help to serve faithfully, managers in need of God's help to steward God's stuff, and peacemakers who experience and extend God's relational grace.

Jesus didn't put a period after the request for daily bread, he put a conjunction. He said, "and." Right after the prayer for daily bread, Jesus tells us to pray for daily debt forgiveness, even as we do the same for others.

That word *debt* is from the financial world. It is something that you owe to someone. It's what financial guru Dave Ramsey doesn't want you to have. People have debt because of their house, their car, their credit cards, and many other things. Debt is a bill you have to pay. Jesus wants us to pray for the forgiveness of our debts and he wants us to pray that daily.

Why? Jesus isn't just trying to humble us, although that certainly happens when we are reminded daily of the ways we have fallen short of the standard we were created for. No, Jesus wants us to walk in a daily

debt-forgiven joy! Because there is nothing quite like the joy after the
debt is gone.

Have you ever paid off a major debt? Many people have. I can't wait to
pay off my home in another 15 years. It's going to be great. Melanie and I
will do our own debt-free Dave Ramsey scream in our front yard.

But you know what would be even greater? Having someone pay off
my debts for me. Have you ever had a major debt paid off by someone
else? Not many have. That's what made what Robert Smith, the billion-
aire, did so uniquely awesome.

In 2019, Smith was the commencement speaker at Morehouse College. And in the midst of his speech, he told the graduating class of 2019
that he was going to pay off all of their student-loan debt. That ended up
being around $34 million worth of student loans paid off!

Can you imagine the joy those students felt when they got the news
that Smith actually followed through and paid off that debt?

The Bible says that all of us have a greater debt than those students
did. We just tend to not feel ultimate realities like we feel financial realities. But the debt is greater.

Jesus' half-brother James says, "Whoever keeps the whole law but fails
in one point has become guilty of all of it" (James 2:10). Did you catch
that? Did you slander someone? Are you greedy or angry? You are as guilty
before God as someone who murdered. That feels weird, but it's because
we don't understand the holiness of God.

We often think about the holiness of God as the part of God that keeps
us from having fun. But it's actually the opposite. The only place where
lasting joy, pleasure, and fun exist is in God's holy presence (Psalm 16:11).
God, in his holiness, looks at our sin as a doctor looks at cancer cells. He
won't be satisfied until all of it is gone. We won't be free until all of it is
removed.

God is more passionate about our daily experience of joy than we
are. As weird as it seems, if you want to become more joyful, you need to
expand your appreciation of God's holiness. When you see him in his holiness, yourself in your sinfulness, and you see what Jesus did to pay the penalty for your sins, it increases your joy—regardless of your circumstances.

Jesus tells us to pray daily for the forgiveness of our debts. But he makes sure that we pray this prayer in a way that shows we have received his past grace. Because his grace always overflows from our heart into the lives of others around us.

He says, "as we also have forgiven our debtors." Jesus doesn't tell us to ask for forgiveness because we have forgiven our debtors. He's not telling us that we can earn God's forgiveness by forgiving others. No. Remember, he's teaching people to pray as children of God, people who have become Christians. His prayer starts with "Our Father in heaven." The saving relationship is already there.

If he's not teaching us to pray in a way that makes us think we can earn his forgiveness, then what is he doing? He wants to make sure that we aren't pro-grace when it comes to our relationship with God, but pro-condemnation when it comes to our relationship with others. The order of the prayer isn't about timing, it's about sincerity. If you could earn his grace, the cross was a waste.

Jesus wants us to know that when God forgives our debts, he deposits debt-forgiving grace in our hearts that we should be using with others. He wants us to understand that when we experience God's grace, we extend God's grace.

Is there anyone you know at home, at work, at church that you need to show some of that debt-relieving grace to?

All of us struggle here. None of us relate to others perfectly. Ken Sande, author of *Resolving Everyday Conflict*, says that people fail to be peacemakers by either being a "peace breaker" or a "peace faker." Peace breakers respond to relational conflict by going into attack mode. Sande says that these people "are more interested in winning a conflict than in preserving a relationship."[22]

Peace fakers respond to relational conflict by trying to escape it. These people deny that it exists or find a way to run away from it. Peace fakers "care more about the appearance of peace than the reality of peace."

Both of these approaches fall short of what God wants for our relationships. Both will find it hard at times to "forgive others' debts." When we are praying for God's kingdom to come and his will to be done in our relationships with others, we are praying for more than these two typical responses. We are praying for God's help to become peacemakers.

Jesus said, "Blessed are the peacemakers, for they shall be called sons of God" (Matthew 5:9). Relational peace doesn't simply happen in our homes, workplace, churches, or anywhere else. It has to be made.

But in order to make peace a reality, we need to understand that we are praying for God's help to do the following three things:

Recognize the wrong—Jesus acknowledges that there are debts that people owe you. Just like a banker, you have people indebted to you. They have wronged you. And God doesn't minimize it. He wants us to know that if they fail one time, it's as if they have failed at every point. It's a big deal. But it's not the final word.

Redirect the punishment—When you forgive a debt, you redirect the punishment, or what is owed for that action, to the cross of Christ. When you forgive, you are saying that Jesus' payment was enough to cover the debt for the sin someone committed against you. When you don't forgive, you say that the cross wasn't enough.

Renew the relationship—Just as your relationship with the bank is changed once the debt is forgiven, your relationship with the guilty party is changed. If the debt is truly forgiven, you don't bring it back up and hold it against the person. While it's true that trust takes time to build back again, forgiveness can happen instantly. And sometimes, when the wrong comes to mind, you need to go to the cross again for a forgiveness payment.

This act of renewing the relationship doesn't mean that the relationship will be the same. There are times where the relationship is over. But it does mean that the bitterness and resentment is gone. It does mean you can pray for that person.

Jesus wants us to be able to pray as the apostle Paul did when everyone left him, but he said, "At my first defense no one came to stand by me, but all deserted me. May it not be charged against them!" (2 Timothy 4:16).

Or, as we struggle to pray for people who have debts they owe us, we can remember Jesus who said from the cross, "'Father, forgive them, for they know not what they do.' And they cast lots to divide his garments" (Luke 23:34).

But perhaps God might call you to pray and take a step of positive engagement. The relational grace that Jesus purchased doesn't only stop the punishment that people deserve, it also provides the fuel to help us become agents of peace, healing, and relational hope. Will it be the same? No. But it can be better with grace that helps grow relationships through difficulty.

How different would our world be if we daily sought out relational grace for our relationship with God and others? The early church united people who were more divided than we are and that had worse histories than we do. His grace can do the same today.

How much time, money, and potential are wasted, how much good, joy, wisdom, and fun are missed out on because families, churches, workplaces, and teams can't forgive? A ton! Let's press into this today.

But we can't do it on our own. We show that we recognize our need for God's help with our relationships when we pray this daily prayer. When we pray this prayer, we signal our understanding that all God's children are called to be peacemakers, using grace as our relational glue. When we allow God's grace to flow through us to others, it provides a glorious picture of something our divided world desperately needs.

Corrie ten Boom knew these truths. In her book *I Stand at the Door and Knock: Meditations by the Author of The Hiding Place*, she wrote, "The wonderful thing about praying is that you leave a world of not being able to do something, and enter God's realm where everything is possible. He specializes in the impossible. Nothing is too great for His almighty power. Nothing is too small for His love."[23]

If you're familiar with her story, you know that these truths come from a deep, authentic place in her heart where she experienced the God who can make peace in any situation. She knew what it was like to struggle to forgive, to ask for God's help, and to move forward into uncharted, glorious, relational territory with God's help.

You see, Corrie ten Boom lived in Holland during World War II. Being in that part of Europe, she was vulnerable to Nazi evil. When she was an adult, she saw Nazis invade her country. Like many others around her, she began to see friends, and especially Jewish friends, disappear.

As a Christian, she didn't sit back and let evil advance. Instead, along with her family, she created a secret compartment, a "hiding place," where they hid Jews until they could find a better place for them.

Others in the area did similar things. In fact, there was a secret network of people doing these things. Around 800 Jewish people were saved through their efforts.

Unfortunately, eventually they were caught and arrested. Corrie and her sister were sent to a concentration camp where they lived in nasty conditions. Even in that place, they tried to share the love of Christ.

Thankfully, Corrie survived, and God used her to tell all kinds of people around the world about their "hiding place." Amazing story.

But there's more.

One night after she finished speaking in Munich, Germany, a man approached her. She recognized the man coming up to her—a former Nazi soldier who stood guard at the shower room door at the concentration camp she had been in. As you might expect, when Corrie saw this former Nazi soldier, terrifying memories came to mind.

He said to her, "How grateful I am for your message...To think that, as you say, He has washed my sins away!" And he extended his hand to shake hers. She tried to raise hers to shake his hand, but she couldn't. She later said:

> I tried to smile, I struggled to raise my hand. I could not. I felt nothing, not the slightest spark of warmth or charity. And so again I breathed a silent prayer. Jesus, I cannot forgive him. Give Your forgiveness. As I took his hand the most incredible thing happened. From my shoulder along my arm and through my hand, a current seemed to pass from me to him, while into my heart sprang a love for this stranger that almost overwhelmed me...When He tells us to love our enemies, He gives, along with the command, the love itself.[24]

Although you haven't spent time in a concentration camp and run into a Nazi guard, my guess is you probably have people in your life that you need Jesus' help forgiving. Former friends? Family members? Strangers? At some point, you'll find yourself feeling as though you can't love others as Jesus wants you to.

Jesus wants us to pray daily for God's help to love others. He wants us to ask for help to forgive others, to make peace where there is a lack of relational peace. And he wants us to travel with God's help to uncharted, glorious relational places that we've never been, whether it's our families, churches, teams, workplace, or whatever.

Will you struggle? Sure. But as you struggle, ask for God's help and reflect on the undeserved forgiveness and love that he poured out on you through Christ. When you are more affected by God's grace than by someone else's sin, you are able to love others as Christ has loved you. Relational wrongs are no longer a place where someone has taken something from you that you can never replace—after all, your heavenly Father doesn't let anyone take something away from you that he thinks is best for you— they become places where the person who has wronged you has given you a unique opportunity to act like the Jesus who forgives and loves the undeserving. That's the kind of love our homes, churches, workplaces, and world need.

DAILY REFLECTION

Do you struggle more with being a peace breaker or a peace faker?

_____

When do you find it hardest to forgive? How can God's grace help you do that?

_____

Why do you think we care more about the small sins others do toward us than the infinitely horrible sins we have done against God?

_____

How might things be better for you, your home, your church,

your workplace if everyone was able to make peace when conflict happened?

_____

What are your "Top Five" relational challenges with others and what would you like God to do in those relationships?

_____

_____

DAILY PRAYER PROMPT

B—Believe God can do anything.
E—Embrace your childlike identity.
S—Specify your requests.
T—Trust God to do what's best with your requests.

DAILY PRAYER

God, thank you for forgiving and loving me when I least deserved it. Thank you for seeing me at my worst and giving me your best. Help me to extend to others what I have received from you in Christ. Make me aware of relational difficulties. Enable me to forgive and love people I think don't deserve it. Help me to love with a long-lasting love. Amen.

What specific requests do you need to make for the roles God's given you today?

Role 1: _____

What you'd like to see God do this week:

_____

Role 2: _____

What you'd like to see God do this week:

_____

Role 3: _____

What you'd like to see God do this week:

_____

Role 4: _____

What you'd like to see God do this week:

_____

Role 5: _____

What you'd like to see God do this week:

_____

Role 6: _____

What you'd like to see God do this week:

_____

Top Four Tasks

1. _____

2. _____

3. _____

4. _____

Top Three Thank-Yous

1. _____

2. _____

3. _____

Today's Two Prayer Texts/Emails

1. _____

2. _____

On-the Go-Prayers

_____

_____

_____

_____

_____

_____

_____

_____

CHILDLIKE PRAYER #5:
PRAYING AS A SOLDIER

Theodon: I will not risk open war.
Aragorn: Open war is upon you whether you would risk it or not.

LORD OF THE RINGS

Lead us not into temptation,
but deliver us from evil.

MATTHEW 6:13

The Lord's Prayer shows us that God's children are worshipers in need of God's help to worship rightly, servants in need of God's help to serve faithfully, managers in need of God's help to steward God's stuff, peacemakers who experience and extend God's relational grace, and finally, soldiers in need of God's help to advance in the spiritual war.

The last request on the Lord's Prayer seems a bit odd when you first read it. It seems as if Jesus is telling us to ask our heavenly Father not to lead us into temptation. The reason that seems odd is that it sounds as if we are asking our holy God to avoid trying to put us in a situation where we'll be tempted and fail. But that's not what's happening.

The word for "temptation" is used 21 times in the New Testament. It can be used positively or negatively. When it is used negatively, it means an "enticement that has the goal of causing one to sin." When it is used positively, it means a test or trial that has as its goal the revealing of the validity of one's faith. Both uses involve a challenge or a test, but they differ in the motivation for that test. Twenty out of the 21 times this word is used it is used in the positive sense. And that's the case here.

Another example of a positive use of the word is found a couple of chapters before this passage, at the beginning of Jesus' temptation. Matthew tells us, "Then Jesus was led up by the Spirit into the wilderness to be tempted by the devil" (Matthew 4:1). Did you catch that? Jesus was led "by the Spirit" into the wilderness why? To be tempted by the devil. The Spirit of God didn't lead Jesus into that situation so that he'd walk out of the wilderness a failure. No, he led him into that challenge so that he'd walk out a victor. The Spirit didn't lead Jesus into the wilderness to fail, he led him into the wilderness because we've failed.

When you understand how this word is used, you can see that this is a prayer that God wouldn't take us into a greater test or trial. We face temptation every day. When we pray this prayer, we are praying that God wouldn't take us into a greater, Matthew 4:1 type of temptation situation.

"But," Jesus says, "deliver us from evil." Rescue us from evil, the evil one, and all its collateral damage we face every day. Jesus is teaching us to pray each day in a way that asks God not to take us into a greater trial today, but that he'd deliver us from the problems and trials we are already in.

When you pray this prayer daily, it changes how you approach your day in four major ways. *First of all*, this prayer reminds us each day that we are in war. Have you ever been on an active battlefield? I haven't, but I've seen enough war movies like *Saving Private Ryan*, *Blackhawk Down*, and all the rest to know that life is different on a battlefield. Your expectations for the day are different. You approach your work, your relationships, and your time all from a different perspective. Jesus uses this daily prayer to remind us that we are in a war.

From Genesis 3 to Revelation 20, the Bible emphasizes the fact that we live in a spiritual war zone. The apostle Peter reminded his readers about this war: "Be sober-minded; be watchful. Your adversary the devil prowls around like a roaring lion, seeking someone to devour" (1 Peter 5:8). The apostle John emphasized this reality too. He said, "We know that we are from God, and the whole world lies in the power of the evil one" (1 John 5:19).

And the battle against evil isn't just external, it's also a battle within. Jesus' half-brother James said, "What causes quarrels and what causes fights among you? Is it not this, that your passions are at war within you?" (James 4:1). Did you catch that? There's a "war within you." Every day, every person on earth has a "war within."

John Piper rightly says, "Until you know that life is war, you cannot know what prayer is for."[25] We are in a war.

But what are we fighting about? We are fighting to hallow the right God in our hearts, to live for God's kingdom, to follow his will in all of our lives, at home, work, and church. But it won't be easy. War never is.

Second, this prayer reminds us that Christians are all on the same team. We are all a part of the same family that is fighting against the enemy. Jesus doesn't teach us to ask that God wouldn't lead just me into temptation or deliver just me from evil. No, Jesus teaches us to pray for us. The prayer is plural. Jesus is using this daily prayer to remind us exactly what the apostle Paul was emphasizing when he said, "Put on the whole armor of God, that you may be able to stand against the schemes of the devil. For we do not wrestle against flesh and blood, but against the rulers, against the authorities, against the cosmic powers over this present darkness, against the spiritual forces of evil in the heavenly places" (Ephesians 6:11-12).

Paul says if you can see them, they're not your enemy. Your friend, coworker, spouse, kids, extended family member, church friend, is not your enemy. They may be hostile to you in certain ways and at certain times, but their behavior doesn't change the truth of God's Word. They are not your enemy.

This truth is easy to understand, but hard to live out. Richard Lovelace, in his book *Dynamics of Spiritual Life: An Evangelical Theology of Renewal*, says, "Although part of the church pays lip service to the reality of sin and worldliness and even demonic agents, it seems to me that much of the church's warfare today is fought by blindfolded soldiers who cannot see the forces ranged against them, who are buffeted by invisible opponents and respond by striking one another."[26]

If you can see them, they're not your enemy. We don't wrestle against flesh and blood. We are in a war and we are on the same team. When you understand that everyone you see is in a battle too, it changes how you treat their failures and frustrations. Soldiers have different relational expectations and sensitivities with other soldiers who they know are being shot at.

Third, this prayer reminds us that we can't handle the enemy. The reason we need to ask for help in this area of life is that we can't handle the enemy on our own. Jesus wants us to understand this not so that we would be frightened, but so that we would be successful. When we are aware of our inabilities in a challenge, we are better prepared to be successful.

Commenting on this passage, nineteenth-century Scottish pastor Alexander Maclaren writes, "The soldier who goes into the field with careful circumspection, knowing the enemy's strength and his own weakness, is the most likely to conquer. It is the presumptuous men, confident in their own strength who are sure to get beaten."[27]

Jesus wants us to pray this prayer daily so that we are better positioned to "win the day" whatever may come our way.

Fourth, this prayer reminds us that the victory belongs to the Lord. You can have hope no matter what you face today because there's nothing your heavenly Father can't handle. He knows what's coming, how to face it, and how to bring you victoriously through it. When you pray this prayer, it shows that you believe that God can handle whatever challenge you are facing or might face.

It reveals that you agree with the apostle John who said, "Little children, you are from God and have overcome them, for he who is in you is greater than he who is in the world" (1 John 4:4).

It shows that your heart is tuned to the truth of Proverbs 21:30-31, which says:

> No wisdom, no understanding, no counsel
>   can avail against the LORD.
> The horse is made ready for the day of battle,
>   but the victory belongs to the LORD.

We need to get our "horses" read for the day of battle, but as we do this, we need to understand that victory belongs to the Lord. We show that we grasp this truth at a heart level when we pray, "deliver us."

As we pray this prayer, it's important that we pray it practically. We need to understand that the battlefields aren't "out there," but they are wherever we are. They are in our homes, our churches, our workplaces, our teams, our culture, and anywhere else we find ourselves.

Jesus teaches us to pray in a way that reminds us each day that we are in a war, that we are on the same team with other Christians, that we aren't strong enough to handle our challenges, and that God is.

C.S. Lewis, one of the leading Christian thinkers of the twentieth century, prefaces his best-selling fiction *The Screwtape Letters* with a few observations about how Christians miss the truth about demonic life. He says, "There are two equal and opposite errors into which our race can fall about the devils. One is to disbelieve in their existence. The other is to believe, and to feel an excessive and unhealthy interest in them."[28] The same tendencies remain today. Some people overlook the influence of demons and others overemphasize it.

Which error are you most prone to make?

Jesus' prayer enables us to avoid both errors. Because Jesus' prayer makes us aware of these evil realities each day, we avoid disbelieving in their existence and, therefore, opening ourselves up to be greatly damaged. Because Jesus' prayer makes us aware of a God who is greater than these evil enemies, we avoid being overly fascinated by them. God is more fascinating, and following him through this battlefield is more exhilarating.

But it's important to ask the question, How can God deliver unholy people who commit evil in his eyes? After all, heaven's definition of evil is much different than ours. Heaven isn't embarrassed by the parts of Scripture that might seem out of step with the culture we live in. The Bible says that we are both victims of evil in the world and perpetrators. How can he deliver us?

Remember the cross of Christ. Jesus can deliver us because he was delivered into the hands of godless men. He took the place of evil humanity on the cross so that he could secure a place for evil humanity in his family.

Have you asked him to deliver you from the penalty of your sin? He always answers that prayer, "Yes"!

But Jesus doesn't just purchase our salvation at the cross. He always defeats the enemy at the cross. The apostle Paul described the cross work of Christ in this way, "He disarmed the rulers and authorities and put them to open shame, by triumphing over them in him" (Colossians 2:15).

At the cross, Jesus defeated the enemy decisively. Victory is secured. But the enemy won't be defeated completely until Jesus returns. As we await that coming day, we must be on guard, alert, and ready for battle. Jesus doesn't want us to take the enemy lightly, "for the devil has come down to you in great wrath, because he knows that his time is short!" (Revelation 12:12). His time is short. His demise is certain. But he's still a serious threat to your daily joy, peace, and purpose. Battle to believe in Christ and his good purposes for you. But remember, like a war, it won't be easy and it won't stay in the area of what you'd expect.

We don't choose our battlefields, our battlefields choose us.

One of the most stunning examples of overcoming the temptations of the enemy on the battlefields we'd never choose comes from the life of Joni Eareckson Tada. Joni was an athletic, overachieving teenager. She was the captain of her lacrosse team. She rode horses on her family's ranch. She made great grades. She had a growing relationship with Jesus, learning about the "abundant life" from John 10 at a Young Life camp. Growing up in Maryland in the fifties and sixties, she seemed to be well on her way to the American Dream.

But everything changed in a moment.

One day, when she was swimming in the Chesapeake Bay, she dove into the water and hit her head. Immediately, she couldn't feel anything in her body. She couldn't move. Her sister had to pull her up. She was screaming that she couldn't move. You can imagine the fear that teenager felt that day.

The following weeks didn't make things easier. Joni had a number of surgeries to try to make things better. Unfortunately, they didn't keep her from becoming a total quadriplegic. She'd never be able to walk again. She ended up spending most of her days lying down, getting flipped every two hours by nurses.

Joni had friends come and share good news with her. They would share Bible verses like Romans 8:28 with her. Joni started to pray for and believe God would heal her miraculously. Sadly, she didn't get healed like she was praying and hoping she would. This new reality led her to struggle with doubt, fear, and depression.

Eventually, as Joni looked to Jesus on the cross, she started to make the best of her new situation. She learned to feed herself again and use a motorized wheelchair. She did all kinds of other things as well.

Today, Joni Eareckson Tada is a world-renowned author and speaker. Her art led her to appear on a number of shows, including *The Today Show.* She carries out her life with a pronounced gratitude and joy.

How can she have that kind of gratitude and joy? It comes from recognizing that she doesn't know what's best for her, but that she has a heavenly Father who does. And he always does what's best for her. Joni trusts her heavenly Father, and we know it because of her joy and gratitude.

Joni powerfully says, "It is a glorious thing to know that your Father God makes no mistakes in directing or permitting that which crosses the path of your life. *It is the glory of God to conceal a matter.* It is *our* glory to trust Him, no matter what."[29]

That's what winning the battle with the enemy in a broken world looks like. The enemy wishes that Joni was ungrateful, resented God, was bitter. But the Spirit of God empowers her to live with more joy and gratitude than many do in our world.

I don't want anyone to go through what Joni went through, but I sure want all of us to have her faith. I pray that all of us can recognize that there is a purpose to our pain and that the most painful parts of our lives are often the most powerful areas of ministry.

DAILY REFLECTION

What evidence have you seen in your life that you are living in a spiritual warzone?

_____

What are your top battlefields? How can you fight more effectively?

_____

Can you see any battlefields in your past that you missed in the moment? How does understanding the spiritual war reality change how you view those past difficulties?

———————————————————————————————

Do you tend to make too much or too little of the enemy's presence? How can you correct that?

———————————————————————————————

Where have you tried to wrestle with "flesh and blood," when God wanted you to fight the unseen enemy by loving the "flesh and blood"? How can you ask God to help you handle those situations differently?

———————————————————————————————

DAILY PRAYER PROMPT

B—Believe God can do anything.
E—Embrace your childlike identity.
S—Specify your requests.
T—Trust God to do what's best with your requests.

DAILY PRAYER

God, deliver me from the darkness. Save me from the darkness around me and within me. Enable me to overcome with joy and gratitude. Amen.

What specific requests do you need to make for the roles God's given you today?

———————————————————————————————

Role 1: _____

What you'd like to see God do this week:

_____

Role 2: _____

What you'd like to see God do this week:

_____

Role 3: _____

What you'd like to see God do this week:

_____

Role 4: _____

What you'd like to see God do this week:

_____

Role 5: _____

What you'd like to see God do this week:

_____

Role 6: _____

What you'd like to see God do this week:

_____

Top Four Tasks

1. _____

2. _____

3. _____

4. _____

Top Three Thank-Yous

1. _____

2. _____

3. _____

Today's Two Prayer Texts/Emails

1. _____

2. _____

On-the-Go Prayers

_____

_____

_____

_____

_____

DAY 21

WEEK 3 COMPLETED! JUST GETTING STARTED

The greatest tragedy of life is not unanswered prayer, but unoffered prayer.

F.B. MEYER

Pray without ceasing.

1 THESSALONIANS 5:17

Way to go! You've made it through week 3!

Over the first week, you learned an approach to prayer that could change your life and the lives of those around you. And you learned that in order to have a prayer life where you see God do awesome things, you don't need to be super spiritual, you just need to be more childlike.

A great prayer life starts with childlike faith in a Father. A great prayer life continues when we embrace our childlike identity. A great prayer life flourishes when we specify our requests like a child. And we can get specific in three primary ways: praying our Bible passages, praying our problems, and praying our plans.

A great prayer life peacefully ends when we, like a child, trust God to do what's best with our request. If we have a God big enough to answer all of our prayers, we have a God who is big enough to have good reasons for not answering our prayers the way we want, but in a way that is best for us. Like the story about my son Judah (see Day 7), if we trust

187

the "who," we'll be able to leave the conversation without the burden we brought into it.

B—Believe God can do anything.

E—Embrace your childlike identity.

S—Specify your requests.

T—Trust God to do what's best with your requests.

Over the second week, you learned the six childlike prayer practices. These practices included prioritizing a private prayer time, writing down your prayers, praying for others in specific ways, praying on the go, fasting with specificity, and remembering that Jesus and the Spirit are praying even when you don't know what to say.

Over the past week, you've learned the five specific childlike identity prayers. You've learned to pray that hearts would hallow the right God, how prayer helps us work in a way that makes a difference, that people would become gospel-centered peacemakers relationally, how Jesus' prayer changes how we view our stuff, and how Jesus' prayer reminds us to battle in the war daily.

Here at the end of the 21-day prayer journey, what prayers has God answered for you and your group? What *nos* has God used to remind you that those weren't what was best for you?

If you keep this up, what might he want to answer in the days ahead? What stories will you have six months from now? I believe there are many.

God can do more in a moment than you can do in a lifetime. Let's ask his help each day to believe that he can do anything, to embrace a childlike identity, to specify our requests, and to trust him to do what's best with our requests.

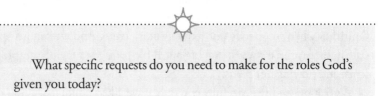

What specific requests do you need to make for the roles God's given you today?

Role 1: _____

What you'd like to see God do this week:

_____

Role 2: _____

What you'd like to see God do this week:

_____

Role 3: _____

What you'd like to see God do this week:

_____

Role 4: _____

What you'd like to see God do this week:

_____

Role 5: _____

What you'd like to see God do this week:

_____

Role 6: _____

What you'd like to see God do this week:

Top Four Tasks

1. _____

2. _____

3._____

4._____

Top Three Thank-Yous

1._____

2._____

3._____

Today's Two Prayer Texts/Emails

1._____

2._____

On-the-Go Prayers

_____

_____

_____

_____

_____

_____

_____

_____

NOTES

1. Paul E. Miller, *A Praying Life: Connecting with God in a Distracting World* (Colorado Springs, CO: NavPress, 2009), 20.

2. J.I. Packer, *Knowing God* (Downers Grove, IL: InterVarsity, 1993), 28-29.

3. Roger Steer, *Spiritual Secrets of George Mueller* (Wheaton, IL: Harold Shaw, 1985), 62.

4. Miller, *A Praying Life*, 23.

5. Tim Keller, *Prayer* (New York: Dutton, 2014), 228.

6. Keller, *Prayer*, 48.

7. Richard J. Foster, *Celebration of Discipline: The Path to Spiritual Growth*, 3rd ed. (New York: HarperCollins, 1998), 48.

8. D. Martyn Lloyd-Jones, *Studies in the Sermon on the Mount*, vol. 1 (Grand Rapids, MI: Eerdmans, 1960), 38.

9. Charles H. Spurgeon, *The Sword and the Trowel* (London: Passmore & Alabaster, 1871), 29.

10. David P. Beaty, *An All-Surpassing Fellowship: Learning from Robert Murray M'Cheyne's Communion with God* (Grand Rapids, MI: Reformation Heritage Books, 2014), 70.

11. Timothy Keller, *Counterfeit Gods: The Empty Promises of Money, Sex, and Power, and the Only Hope That Matters* (New York: Dutton, 2009), xvii.

12. As cited in Iain H. Murray, *Heroes* (Carlisle, PA: The Banner of Truth Trust, 2009), 30.

13. As cited in Murray, *Heroes*, 81.

14. Augustine, *Confessions* (Oxford, England: Oxford University Press, 1991), 181.

15. Augustine, *Confessions, 3.*

16. Graeme Goldsworthy, *Gospel and Kingdom* (Exeter, England: Paternoster, 1981), 47.

17. Lawrence Elliott, *George Washington Carver: The Man Who Overcame* (Englewood Cliffs, NJ: Prentice-Hall, 1966), 156.

18. Randy Alcorn, *Money, Possessions, and Eternity*, revised and updated (Carol Stream, IL: Tyndale, 2003), 19.

19. Alcorn, *Money, Possessions, and Eternity*, 140.

20. Janet Benge, *George Mueller: Guardian of Bristol's Orphans* (Seattle, WA: YWAM, 1999), 196.

21. Alcorn, *Money, Possessions, and Eternity*, 254.

22. Ken Sande and Kevin Johnson, *Resolving Everyday Conflict* (Grand Rapids, MI: Baker, 2011), 39.

23. Corrie ten Boom, *The Hiding Place* (Grand Rapids, MI: Baker, 2011), 246-247.

24. Randy Alcorn, *Truth: A Bigger View of God's Word* (Eugene, OR: Harvest House, 2017), 16.

25. John Piper, *Let the Nations Be Glad: The Supremacy of God in Missions* (Grand Rapids, MI: Baker, 1993), 49.

26. Richard Lovelace, *Dynamics of Spiritual Life: An Evangelical Theology of Renewal* (Downers Grove, IL: InterVarsity, 1979), 18.

27. Alexander Maclaren, *Expositions of Holy Scripture*, vol. 4 (Grand Rapids, MI: Eerdmans, 1959), 282.

28. C.S. Lewis, *The Screwtape Letters* (New York: Simon & Schuster, 1996), 15.

29. Joni Eareckson Tada, *Glorious Intruder* (Portland, OR: Multnomah, 1989), 173.

To learn more about Harvest House books and
to read sample chapters, visit our website:

www.HarvestHousePublishers.com

HARVEST HOUSE PUBLISHERS
EUGENE, OREGON